Creating Learning
Places for
Teachers, Too

Total Quality Education for the World's Best Schools

The Comprehensive Planning and Implementation Guide for School Administrators

Series Editor: Larry E. Frase

The authors dedicate this series to the memory of
W. Edwards Deming, 1900-1993

Creating Learning Places for Teachers, Too

Larry E. Frase
Sharon C. Conley

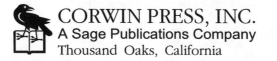

CORWIN PRESS, INC.
A Sage Publications Company
Thousand Oaks, California

For information address:

Corwin Press, Inc.
A Sage Publications Company
2455 Teller Road
Thousand Oaks, California 91320

SAGE Publications Ltd.
6 Bonhill Street
London EC2A 4PU
United Kingdom

SAGE Publications India Pvt. Ltd.
M-32 Market
Greater Kailash I
New Delhi 110 048 India

Printed in the United States of America

Library of Congress Cataloging-in-Publication Data

Frase, Larry E.
    Creating learning places for teachers, too / Larry E. Frase, Sharon C. Conley.
        p. cm.—(Total quality education for the world's best schools; v. 3)
    Includes bibliographical references.
    ISBN 0-8039-6121-9 (pbk. : alk. paper)
    1. Teacher participation in administration—United States.
    2. School management and organization—United States. 3. Total
    quality management—United States. 4. Educational change—United
    States. I. Conley, Sharon C. II. Title. III. Series.
    LB2806.45 F73 1994   94-388
    371.2—dc20

94 95 96 97 10 9 8 7 6 5 4 3 2 1

Corwin Production Editor: Yvonne Könneker

✧　　✧

Contents

Foreword

One of the primary tenets of the quality movement has been the need to keep a keen eye on who the customer really is. In this book, Larry Frase and Sharon Conley state that schools' greatest resource is teachers, their human capital. Further, they propound the belief that teachers, too, must be considered customers. Frase and Conley pursue the point that unless teachers are included in this provocative concept, it will be impossible to attain and sustain quality improvement in education. In turn, all persons in the organization must look downstream to determine who their customers are. Superintendents must view assistant superintendents as customers, assistant superintendents must view principals as customers, and principals must view teachers as customers. The authors postulate that this practice is necessary to remove the roadblocks that hinder educational progress. People at every level must deliver quality to their customers.

Frase and Conley contend that giving and receiving constructive feedback are hallmarks of Total Quality Education (TQE) schools. They present research data that reveal the lack of constructive feedback given to teachers and principals on their work. Old-style evaluation systems rank people and reduce motivation. The failure of such evaluation systems and management's motivation methods is clearly illustrated in what Frase and Conley call self-exhausting systems. In contrast, they describe quality renewal systems, which are based on the positive effects of constructive feedback and the relationships among satisfaction, motivation, and work.

Frase and Conley make it abundantly clear that in the old kind of school management, "shared decision making" is an anachronism; that is, under such management, the principal makes the decisions and the staff "shares in them." School administrative practices must move toward a consensual model in which teachers are considered equal with principals. Frase and Conley point out that this model is not one of simple majority rule, for such procedures often violate the rights of the minority and undermine progress. Rather, what is really changed in a TQE school is the position of the principal as an "authority figure." Under a TQE approach, the principal is much more likely to say, "We were concerned about this, and after discussion we reached a consensus that we should proceed with the action you see."

A new kind of dialogue erupts in TQE schools, and Frase and Conley's experience in teaching, administration, and research unfolds in this book to provide the theory, tools, and clues as to its sources, substance, form, and evolution. One thing is clear: It is a dialogue, and not a monologue in disguise. Readers should know that the attitude toward change is more important than the content it may embrace. An administrator determined to understand and become part of TQE has already adopted the most important position of all.

Fenwick W. English
University of Kentucky

✧   ✧

Preface

We have devoted much of our professional energies in the past few years to reading, conducting research, consulting, and writing about the topics addressed in this book. Our focus has always been on maximizing the power and effectiveness of schoolteachers, the human capital of education. As we pooled and debated the content and premises of this book, it became clear to us that our concerns are very well summarized by Seymour Sarason (1990): "It is virtually impossible to create and sustain over time conditions for productive learning for students when they do not exist for teachers" (p. 145).

This book advances the premise that teachers, too, in addition to students, must be viewed as customers of the school. Unfortunately, schools have generally failed to operate on this premise. Designing, developing, and maintaining a creative, high-energy learning environment takes tremendous vigor and skill. No one can accomplish this continually when isolated in his or her work and deprived of new learning, skills enhancement, and academic stimulation. Schools have failed to unleash the tremendous potential of teachers for educating young people. This is evidenced in student achievement scores, high teacher attrition rates, and record numbers of teachers reporting burnout.

We believe that teachers are every school's greatest resource, and that only through teachers' professional growth and development can schools achieve marked success. This thesis addresses redesigning teachers' jobs and work environments so that they offer teachers maximum potential for developing maximum motivation and satisfaction in teaching. Old methods, such as autocratic supervision, bureaucratic top-down decision making, isolation, personnel evaluation by inspection, and exhortations and threats to work harder, have not been successful in the past and they will not be successful in the future. Such methods have been harmful; they have retarded the development of teaching as a profession. They conflict with new knowledge about how people learn and develop motivation.

In this book, we present the new premises that are needed and practical ideas for implementing them in schools. The new premises are as follows:

- Satisfaction and motivation are the results of successful work.
- The benefits of quick-fix, extrinsic rewards will be short-lived.
- Everyone has a right to experience joy in his or her work.
- It is administrators' responsibility to facilitate the creation of a work environment where teachers can achieve success and experience joy in work.
- Teachers desire and can benefit greatly from accurate, constructive feedback.
- The intrinsic rewards found in work are far more powerful motivators than are extrinsic rewards.
- Teachers, like other professionals, willingly emulate the qualities leaders model and reject words that conflict with leaders' actions.
- Giving support to others to achieve success results in greater success for all.
- Professional development is one of the most powerful routes to teacher motivation and school improvement.
- The focus of schools must be narrowed, and constancy of purpose must be maintained.

These premises constitute the thesis of this book—that teachers must be considered as customers. They are derived from what we believe is the most salient knowledge gathered over the past 40 years. We readily admit that many of the ideas in this book are not ours. They come from the work of many theorists and practitioners, including W. Edwards Deming, Hackman and Oldham, and Porter and Lawler, as indicated by the many references in the text. We ourselves have written previously about many aspects of the thesis and premises presented here, in *Maximizing People Power in Schools* (Frase, 1992a), *The School as a Work Environment: Implications for Reform* (Conley & Cooper, 1991), *School Management by Wandering Around* (Frase, 1990), *Teacher Compensation and Motivation* (Frase, 1992b), and *When Teachers Participate in School Decisions* (Conley & Rables, 1993).

The topic of creating learning places for teachers covers much ground. Because of this we divided responsibility for writing the chapters as follows:

Chapters 1, 2, 4, and 6—Larry Frase

Chapters 3 and 5 (with contributions from L. Frase)—Sharon Conley

The guiding premises may seem radical, and they may constitute paradigm shifts for many school administrators. Now more than ever, change is needed. School choice initiatives are being pushed onto ballots in many states. What was a monopolistic hold on schooling will deteriorate in a free market. We offer this book as a source of ideas for instituting substantive improvements in the public schools, and hence to ensure for their continued existence.

Redesigning schools around these premises may be difficult, but paradigm pioneers know that. As assistance to the pioneers who set out to create Total Quality Education schools, we offer theoretical background and day-to-day practices for busting old, outdated, and ineffective paradigms as they apply to human capital, teachers. We intend this book to be helpful to teachers, administrators, and board members in redesigning the workplace and personnel management practices. The goal is to maximize the potential of education's most valuable resource, the teacher.

We hope you find this book easy to read and comprehend, and highly practical. Let us turn now to the task at hand.

Larry E. Frase
San Diego State University

Sharon C. Conley
University of Maryland at College Park

References

Conley, S., & Robles, J. (1993). When teachers participate in school decisions. In T. Astuto (Ed.), *When teachers lead*. University Park, PA: University Council for Education Administration.

Conley, S. C., & Cooper, B. C. (1991). *The school as a work environment: Implications for reform*. Boston: Allyn & Bacon.

Frase, L. E. (1990). *School management by wandering around*. Lancaster, PA: Technomic.

Frase, L. E. (1992a). *Maximizing people power in schools*. Newbury Park, CA: Corwin.

Frase, L. E. (1992b). *Teacher compensation and motivation*. Lancaster, PA: Technomic.

Sarason, S. B. (1990). *The predictable failure of school reform*. San Francisco: Jossey-Bass.

✧   ✧

About the Authors

Larry E. Frase is Professor of Educational Administration at San Diego State University. He has 16 years experience in school administration, including 6 years as Assistant Superintendent and 8 as Superintendent. He completed his master's degree and his doctorate at Arizona State University. He has published 50 articles in professional journals. *School Management by Wandering Around* (1990) is used in graduate courses and by practicing school administrators. His book *Motivating and Compensating Teachers* (1992) is becoming a hallmark in the educational arena. His most recent book is *Maximizing People Power in Schools* (1992). He has served as a speaker and/or consultant for more than 75 state and national conferences, school districts, and universities. He has received numerous honors and awards at professional conferences and was selected as one of the Top One Hundred School Administrators in the United States by the National School Board Association and the American Association of School Administrators.

Sharon C. Conley received her Ph.D. from the University of Michigan. She is Associate Professor of Administration and Supervision in the Department of Education Policy, Planning, and Administration at the University of Maryland at College Park. Her writing and research interests are in the general areas of organizational behavior in administration. She has written numerous articles on the topics of school organization and management, teacher career development, teacher participation in decision making, and work redesign. Her book, *The School as a Work Environment: Implications for Reform* (1991) brought together leading experts who are examining all aspects of the school as a workplace.

✧ 1 ✧

Students and Teachers as Customers

We wrote this book based on our conviction that both students and teachers are customers of school systems. Further, this book is based on the premise that efforts to improve schooling for students will continue to be marginally effective until teachers are given the same level of consideration as students. To think that teachers can create and sustain creative, dynamic learning environments for others without having the same for themselves is folly. We know of no industry or school that has found a way to look after external customers successfully (e.g., students) while abusing internal customers (e.g., teachers and administrators). As Peters and Waterman (1982) suggest, the process of meeting customer needs begins internally.

The public education system in the United States was designed to ensure a literate society. Thus, justifiably, students became the primary focus of the schools. Through the years, the list of responsibilities schools must fulfill has grown rapidly. The aim of the first schools was primarily to teach reading, but as the list of subjects to be taught grew longer and longer, so did the schools' social obligations. For example, schools today must ensure racial integration, gender equity, equity of educational offerings, and medical care, and must offer parenting classes, free breakfast and lunch programs, environmental education, sex education, and AIDS education. All of these responsibilities are important; none should be omitted. All are vital to the growth and development of youth and a healthy society. Great care is taken in the schools to provide stimulating environments for students, to promote learning. And it is the job of teachers and administrators to do these things.

The above list represents no mean chore. It is gigantic, and conditions in many schools, particularly urban schools, are appalling. As the demands on teachers have multiplied, support from parents and social agencies has declined. Beginning and experienced teachers' number-one goal is to educate students successfully. For teachers to achieve this goal, the educational system must view both teachers and their students as internal customers. Teachers educate students, and this happens in classrooms, not in superintendents' or principals' offices. As Deming (1986) states, "The people who make the product are the only ones who can ensure high quality" (p. 49). Central office administrators must look downstream to principals and serve them, instead of viewing principals as their servants. In turn, principals must view teachers as customers, and determine how they can best help teachers do the job of teaching. Every administrator must realize that teachers' successes are greatly dependent on the quality of their work environments. It is the administrators' job to clear the schools of the many obstacles that stand in the way of teachers' achieving their number-one goal, helping students learn successfully. The view that administrators are superior to everyone below them on the organizational chart, and that their job is simply to require work of subordinates, must be changed; administrators at all levels need to work to facilitate the teacher's job. Jan Carlzon, chief executive officer of Scandinavian Airlines, has said it very well: "If you're not serving the customer, your job is to be serving someone who is" (quoted in Anderson & Zemke, 1991, p. 31).

A basic tenet of Total Quality Management (TQM) is that 85% of the problems in an organization are caused by the systems operating within the organization; only 15% are caused by the people. For Total Quality Education (TQE), this suggests that we should devote our time and energies to ferreting out problems and inefficiencies in the system, rather than focusing on teacher and principal evaluation only. Every person in the school system should focus on delivering the very best product to the next person, forget quotas, and concentrate on improving the systems and work environment. When this is accomplished, many problems previously attributed to people will be resolved, because the systems will optimize the contributions of teachers, custodians, aides, and administrators. Administrators will go from being inspectors and managers to providers and helpers for teachers. Teachers will change from bureaucratic servants to educators, and both teachers and students will be viewed as the internal customers of the school system. As servants/leaders, supervisors will be devoted to clearing schools and their systems of obstacles that hinder learning.

We contend that until teachers are supported in developing a work environment equal to the one they are required to provide for their students, efforts to improve schools and ultimately the education of students will continue to be marginally successful, at best. That is what this book is about, creating work environments where teachers can learn, grow, and improve the quality of their teaching, where teachers and students are customers. Schools are for teachers, too. Let's get started.

Constancy of Purpose

Constancy of purpose is crucial to success in all organizations (Deming, 1986). This concept has two highly important meanings for schools:

1. Maintain the focus of the organization. Don't jump from one purpose to another without ensuring that whatever is proposed fits the school's mission.
2. Focus constantly on improving the quality of the system within which teachers must teach and students must learn.

Schools are often led astray from their missions by activist groups, legislation, school boards, and administrators who want to promote the latest trend. This topic is covered in depth in another volume in this series, *Making Governance Work: TQE for School Boards* (Poston, 1994). The best way for a school or district to avoid these distractions and keep on track is to have in place a formal mission statement, along with action plans to accomplish it. If a school's mission is unknown or not shared, defining it can fall to anyone who takes the time and energy to do it. The intricacies of developing a shared mission statement and planning documents are explained very well elsewhere (Scheetz & Benson, 1994; Kaufman, 1992). The point is that successful school principals and superintendents determine what results the public expects and needs and establish clear priorities for achieving those results. As Joel Barker (1991) has said so well, "Vision [read as mission] without action is dreaming. Action without vision is random activity. Vision and action together can change the world." In the remainder of this book we address the need for administrators to create constancy of purpose, the actions they must take for schools, and how they can work with teachers and other staff to accomplish a shared mission.

Because we believe that 85% of problems in schools are attributable to systems, and not individuals, we focus on the quality of the systems in schools and school districts, not on individuals' skills and performance. Our goal is to improve the systems in which teachers work, as well as the skill level of teachers. The quality of student learning cannot be greater than the quality of the systems in the schools and other environments in which teachers must teach. Constant efforts are needed on both fronts before substantive improvements can be made in the quality of education.

In this book, we present the principal as a leader who successfully encourages and provides opportunities for teachers also to lead. The principal, then, is a leader of leaders. Principals, as leaders, cannot improve schools by themselves; leadership and school improvement require a team effort on the part of administrators and teachers, who work in close contact with the schools' primary customers, students. In general, there are three ways to achieve goals (Scherkenbach, 1991):

- Dependently, allowing oneself to be swept along
- Independently, working without regard for others
- Interdependently, working cooperatively with others or competing with others

Obviously, only one of these possibilities is adequate. Being swept along is being adrift, not providing leadership; the power of a school or any organization is in its people working together with concern, not without concern, for each other and the school's mission. Competition has not been shown to be an effective way to motivate people (Kohn, 1986), but cooperative work results in high-quality productivity and pride and joy in work.

In this book we address the conception of the leader as servant, or follower. In this context, the principal is a person who continually looks for ways to improve the systems within the school, in consultation with others who have impacts on the school. The successful principal works to ensure that the school's environment promotes learning for students and teachers through Total Quality Education (TQE). Some have told us that the notion of the principal as servant degrades the principal's importance as leader, but we do not hold this view at all. TQE does not minimize leadership; rather, it recognizes that leadership and support from top management are central to optimization of the system. This book is based on the belief that the principal is the key to the TQE school. The principal is the reason teachers either thrive or wither in a school. Boyer (1983) summarizes it well: "In schools where achievement was high and where there was a clear sense of community, we found, invariably, that the principals make the difference" (p. 219).

To make TQE the operating style in schools, the view of principals as bosses must be transformed; principals must be seen as filling facilitation and support roles for systems and as creating high-quality work environments that enhance teaching and learning. TQE principals believe that teachers want to do a good job teaching and that custodians want to keep schools safe and clean. TQE principals foster teachers' desires to learn and develop their career goals by continually improving the system and providing training resources. The first step in the transformation is for everyone in the system to manage him- or herself better and to appraise him- or herself based on what others need (Deming, 1993). Such self-appraisal can begin to convert the belief that principals must inspect teachers to the belief that teachers share the vision and do the teaching while principals orchestrate the shared vision and ensure a productive work environment and adequate resources. TQM offers a very straightforward principle for this: "Put everybody in the company to work to accomplish the transformation" (Deming, 1992).

The Self-Exhausting System

Many ineffective schools are guided by what we call the self-exhausting system (SES). The SES feeds off its employees by relying on extrinsic rewards for motivation. The result is inevitably exhaustion and failure for the organization and the people in it. The leaders of schools in which self-exhausting systems are at work are not dastardly Darth Vader types; they simply do not know better.

As illustrated in Figure 1.1, the SES may yield job satisfaction and motivation, but only briefly and in very small amounts. The inadequacy of the SES lies in the following assumptions:

- External rewards offer greater motivation potential than internal rewards.
- People must be bribed with extrinsic rewards, cajoled, or intimidated into doing their work (Theory X).
- Work is worthwhile because of the extrinsic rewards it delivers.

For years, in both industry and education, workers have struck for higher pay and improved benefits. An experience one of the authors had in the early 1970s, as assistant superintendent in a heavily unionized school district on Long Island, serves as an illustration of the SES at work. Negotiations were at an impasse, with the local American Federation of Teachers (AFT) teacher representatives, and the board deadlocked over salary issues. Subsequently, the board agreed to an unprecedented 15% increase to the salary schedule. Teachers were appreciative and their association communicated that the fair settlement meant that teachers could now concentrate on teaching and its rewards. They did—for

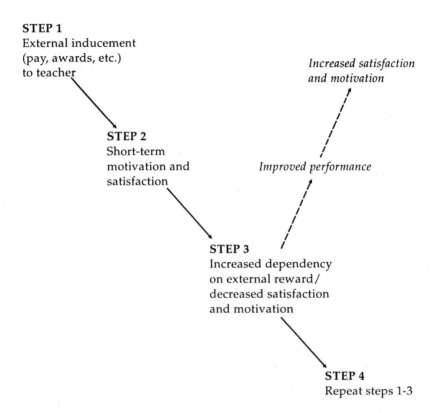

Figure 1.1. The Self-Exhausting System

two months. Come the first of October, teachers expressed disappointment about the management process. Grievances were filed. Complaints of unfair labor practices were filed. And communication between teachers and administrators halted. The feelings of satisfaction on the part of teachers, their leaders, and administrators vanished, and when negotiations began the following spring, teachers and administrators were divided. Teacher representatives and managers then focused mostly on pay issues, providing less attention to other underlying causes of job dissatisfaction. The scenario repeated itself. Association leaders and teachers expressed satisfaction over pay increases, but grievance filing began again in October.

Let's examine two very important facts here. First, the salary paid to beginning teachers in the district ranged from $23,000 to $40,000 (depending on the location) with full medical, dental, and retirement benefits. This was an attractive package, especially in 1973. Second, most teachers in the district were at or near the top of the salary schedule, but many were dissatisfied with the managerial work environment they faced in their schools.

Both the association leaders and the school board were doing what they thought was right. They were convinced Theory X was *the* answer. Negotiations focused on bread and butter issues as the most important consideration, giving insufficient attention to other aspects of the work environment that teachers faced. This scenario is a real-life example of an SES. Let's follow the steps in Figure 1.1 using this case:

- *Step 1:* Extend extrinsic inducement to teachers. (Both the union and the board focused on extrinsic motivators.)
- *Step 2:* Reap the result of short-term satisfaction minus increased motivation or improved performance. (Teachers demonstrated satisfaction for only 1 or 2 months and showed no evidence of instructional improvement.)
- *Step 3:* Expectations for and dependence on extrinsic rewards are strengthened. (Without seeking a deeper form of satisfaction, such as intrinsic satisfaction, the union and board again relied on extrinsic rewards to satisfy and motivate the teachers. The strategy worked no better the second time than it had the first time.)
- *Step 4:* Focus is further removed from internal motivation, and satisfaction decreases. (The dependence on extrinsic rewards increases each time Steps 2 and 3 are repeated, and energies are depleted in the exhaustive struggle for external rewards.)
- *Step 5:* Repeat Steps 1-4.

In the SES the teachers are exhausted and drained of the inherent drive of teaching—helping others learn is lost when the focus is on extrinsic rewards.

The overriding point here is that teachers and most other people have financial requirements. Once these requirements are reasonably well accommodated, however, increased accommodation does not yield job satisfaction or motivation to improve skills or career development. Teachers in the SES are exhausted by the nearly constant conflict and turmoil created in the fight to attain more and more extrinsic rewards. The benefit of intrinsic rewards is lost or heavily masked. As shown in Figure 1.2, performance and satisfaction decline as the constant struggle for extrinsic rewards increases.

The Quality Renewal System

Employment of the quality renewal system (QRS) characterizes effective schools. The QRS focuses not on extrinsic rewards, but on what the French philosopher Bergson called *élan vital*, the original vital impetus that is the substance of consciousness and nature (see Baumer, 1977), the vital drive to do good in one's life. The QRS melds *élan vital* with a workplace that enables teachers to do their best, one that removes impediments to success.

The QRS is based on practices developed from major research findings over the past 40 years (e.g., Hackman & Oldham, 1980; Herzberg, Mausner, & Snyderman, 1959; Sergiovanni, 1967), which provide formidable evidence of the following:

- People want to do their jobs well.
- When successful, people take pride and satisfaction in their work.
- People are motivated to develop their careers and improve their skills.
- People are satisfied by the result of work, not the cause of it. Satisfaction is the result of good work.
- People must have their financial and security needs met before they can maximize their career development and job performance, satisfaction, and motivation.

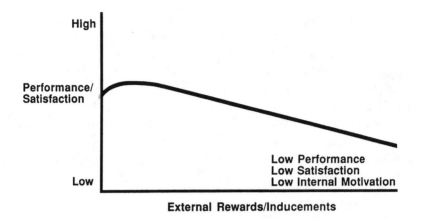

Figure 1.2. Relation Between Extrinsic Inducement/Rewards and Performance/Satisfaction

The QRS is the embodiment of TQE, TQM, the evidence just cited, and the belief in the special *élan vital* possessed by teachers. Quality renewal systems strongly reflect Deming's (1993) belief that continual improvement is crucial to and synonymous with organizations' success and workers' desires to contribute by doing the best job possible.

The QRS invests its resources in its people and the systems with which they work, because it is based on the belief that people's work can be no better than the quality of the systems with which they work. (In Chapter 4, we address the importance of involving teachers in improving the systems in which they work.) The results are improved quality of work and enhanced pride and joy in work. As illustrated in Figure 1.3, the steps of the QRS are as follows:

- *Step 1:* Provide internal rewards as inducements. For educators, such inducements include teachers' desire to help others learn, improved systems that enable teachers to improve education for students, improved instructional skills, and motivation for career development.
- *Step 2:* Improved performance.

- *Step 3:* Increased job satisfaction and increased motivation to improve skills and the work system further results.
- *Step 4:* Repeat Steps 1-3.

The QRS is self-renewing. Improved success on the job comes from improved systems and job skills. Success results in continual renewal of job satisfaction and motivation to make further improvements in the system and personal work skills.

There is another vital assumption: Basic financial and security needs must be met before QRS can work effectively. Adequate supplies of money are crucial to meeting these needs. Money serves to prevent job dissatisfaction, but, as illustrated in Figure 1.1, it will not produce job satisfaction, motivation, or improved quality of work. These can be attained only through intrinsic motivators. Improved job performance and confidence yield greater motivation to seek further improvement. Doing the job better becomes the goal in the QRS. In contrast to the diminishing returns produced by extrinsic motivators (see Figure 1.2), the QRS yields continually increasing satisfaction and the drive to make further improvements. This is illustrated in Figure 1.4.

Teachers as Customers

Although schools have been built expressly for students, it is incumbent upon everyone in the organization to treat every other person as a customer, too. Board members, administrators, and teachers must look upstream *and* downstream to determine what is needed to deliver the highest-quality products possible: well-educated students. Board members must set directions for the district and then clear the district of impediments to working in those directions. In like fashion, central office administrators must provide resources and assistance to principals so that they can do their jobs. Principals in turn must view teachers as their customers. They must continually improve the systems that affect teachers' work. Further, they must provide work settings where teachers can successfully teach their students and thereby gain

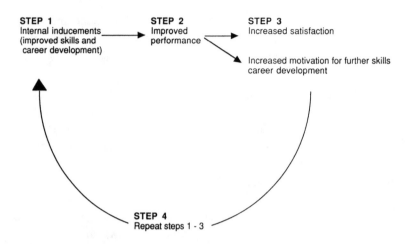

Figure 1.3. The Quality Renewal System

the resulting satisfaction and motivation to improve their skills and enhance their career development. This is the QRS.

The TQE principal engages everyone in improving the school. He or she encourages teachers to lead and supports teachers with resources. The TQE leader is not a high-profile personality. Improving the systems in the school, gaining the participation of all staff, and providing resources for career development are of primary importance. The TQE principal possesses an intuitive understanding of the delicate balance between the performance of every staff member and the quality of the systems staff members use. In doing so, the principal's aim is to provide the necessities and resources that will allow teachers to find joy in work. The following quotation from the Chinese philosopher Lao-tzu (1944) captures the essence of the TQE principal/leader:

> A leader is best
> When people barely know that he exists,
> Not so good when people obey and acclaim him,
> worst when they despise him.
> Fail to honor people, they fail to honor you;
> But of a good leader, who talks little,

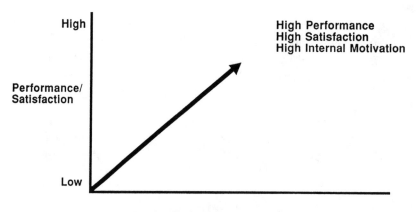

Figure 1.4. Relation Between Intrinsic Inducements/Rewards and Performance/Satisfaction

When his work is done, his aim fulfilled,
They will all say, We did this ourselves.

In the remaining chapters, we offer some tools crucial to the QRS and to TQE leaders.

Key Terms and Concepts

Constancy of purpose. In this context, the dual focus on human and material resources of the school and constant improvement of the system within which teachers teach and students learn.

Élan vital. The vital force people possess that motivates them to do good in their lives.

Extrinsic inducements. Outward, physical rewards, such as money, given to employees (teachers and principals) for both compensation and motivation.

Intrinsic inducements. Inward, basic rewards, such as job satisfaction, found in schools where quality renewal systems are in place.

Quality renewal system. A system that constantly strives to im-prove systems and job skills through a focus on intrinsic induce-ments; continually renews employees' (teachers and principals) success as the prime motivator for improved performance and systems.

Self-exhausting system. A system, typical of many schools, in which extrinsic rewards are used to motivate educators; the result is exhaustion and failure for the organization and the people in it.

References

Anderson, K., & Zemke, R. (1991). *Delivering knock your socks off service.* New York: AMACOM, American Management Asso-ciation.

Barker, J. (1991). *Discovering the future: The business of paradigms* (2nd ed.) [videotape]. Burnsville, MN: Charthouse Learning Corporation.

Baumer, F. (1977). *Modern European thought.* New York: Macmillan.

Boyer, E. L. (1983). *High school: A report on secondary education in America.* New York: Harper & Row.

Deming, W. E. (1986). *Out of the crisis.* Cambridge, MA: MIT Center for Advanced Engineering Study.

Deming, W. E. (1992, October). *Quality, productivity, and competitive position.* Paper presented at the Quality Enhancement Semi-nars, Los Angeles.

Deming, W. E. (1993). *The new economics for industry, government, education.* Cambridge, MA: MIT Center for Advanced Engi-neering Study.

Hackman, J., & Oldham, G. (1980). *Work redesign.* Menlo Park, CA: Addison-Wesley.

Herzberg, F., Mausner, B., & Snyderman, B. (1959). *The motivation to work.* New York: John Wiley.

Kaufman, R. (1992). *Mapping educational success.* Newbury Park, CA: Corwin.

Kohn, A. (1986). *No contest.* Boston: Houghton Mifflin.

Lao-tzu. (1944). *The way of life* (W. Brynner, Trans.). New York: Perigee.

Peters, T. J., & Waterman, R. H., Jr. (1982). *In search of excellence.* New York: Harper & Row.

Poston, W. K., Jr. (1994). *Making governance work: TQE for school boards.* Thousand Oaks, CA: Corwin.

Scheetz, M. & Benson, T., (1994). *Structuring schools for success: A view from the inside.* Thousand Oaks, CA: Corwin.

Scherkenbach, W. W. (1991). *Deming's road to continual improvement.* Knoxville, TN: SPC.

Sergiovanni, T. J. (1967). Factors which affect satisfaction and dissatisfaction of teachers. *Journal of Educational Administration, 5,* 66-82.

✧ 2 ✧

Motivating Through
Profound Knowledge

Educators easily recognize the differences between motivated and unmotivated teachers when we observe their classrooms, see them work in groups with other teachers, and observe them in faculty meetings. Motivated teachers are enthusiastic, skilled, happy to share knowledge and wisdom with their learners, and happy to share their success with fellow teachers. We all have known teachers who have experienced great joy from teaching. Taoist scholar Chuang Tzu referred to this euphoric state as *Yu*. *Yu* is a synonym for the right way of following the path, or *Tao*, which has been translated into English as wandering, as walking without touching the ground, or as swimming, flying, and flowing. Tzu believed that *Yu* was the proper way to live—without concern for external rewards, spontaneously, with total commitment. Tzu was not referring to hedonistic pleasure, but to the enjoyment of the active command of a skill and the spirit that comes from that enjoyment. When students learn with pleasure and teachers teach with pleasure, the essential aspects of the TQE school have been attained. In Japan, this is called *ikigai*—that which makes life worth living.

The difficult questions concern why some teachers are motivated and others are not, and how we can go about motivating teachers so that they will derive pleasure, satisfaction, confidence, and ultimately increased motivation from teaching. We are aware, as administrators, that fundamental changes must occur before we can substantially improve our educational system. But wanting to make such improvement is not enough—we must know precisely what we want to accomplish, what to do to achieve it, and how to do it. Deming (1992) has identified four areas of "profound knowledge," knowledge that is crucial to building a workplace in which there is potential for workers to find motivation. To use profound knowledge, we must transform our current management style into one in keeping with TQE. In this chapter, we discuss the following eight areas of profound knowledge:

- Appreciation for a system
- Knowledge of variation
- Theory of knowledge
- Knowledge of psychology
- Flow, the optimal experience
- Autotelic jobs
- Abundance and scarcity mentality
- Efficacy and locus of control

None of these eight areas stands alone; all of them are systemic, interconnected, interdependent. A change in one affects all the others. The TQE literature provides the first four areas listed here; we have added the last four. These eight areas of profound knowledge are the keys to decision making in TQE schools.

Appreciation for a System

A school, as a system, is made up of internal customers (students, teachers, administrators), external customers (parents, other community members, community businesses and industry), and all processes and procedures working together to accomplish the mission of the school. In TQE language, the orchestration of the efforts of all these components of a school toward achieving the school's mission is called *optimization*. When the school's purpose is achieved, every person involved with the school benefits. Every person in the system is dependent upon every other person for achieving success. Only when the school is successful (optimized) will all the professionals in the school be successful, and vice versa.

When a system is not optimized—that is, when it is *suboptimized*—everybody in the system loses. For those of us in education, this simply means that when children learn, we all benefit. Student growth and development are inextricably tied to teacher motivation and satisfaction.

Appreciation for a system includes having a mission; understanding the interconnectedness and interdependence of internal and external customers and all components, processes, and procedures; and maintaining constancy of purpose. We discuss these elements below.

Having a Mission

There can be no system without a mission. Without a mission the people in the school are simply flailing, attempting to keep their heads above water, going nowhere, and expending valuable resources. The importance of a mission statement to an organization's success has been highlighted for more than 30 years. Sadly, many mission statements are woefully vague or so grandiose that they communicate little and no one takes them seriously. Few are of sufficient quality to guide a school or district.

Mission statements for human systems such as schools should reflect the values of the lay and educational communities in which the schools are found. The finest mission statement we have seen is the following:

The mission of the New Rochelle School System, acknowledging its richly complex history, is to produce responsible, self-sufficient citizens who possess the self-esteem, initiative, skills, and wisdom to continue individual growth, pursue knowledge, develop aesthetic sensibilities, and value cultural diversity by providing intellectually challenging educational programs that celebrate change but affirm tradition and promote excellence through an active partnership with the community, a comprehensive and responsive curriculum, and a dedicated and knowledgeable staff. (quoted in Sarason, 1990, p. 155)

This mission statement has two crucial ingredients:

1. It identifies the importance of teamwork between two major stakeholders, the community and the staff, in attaining the mission.
2. It strongly emphasizes the overarching goal of engendering and sustaining in students a desire "to continue individual growth, pursue knowledge, [and] develop aesthetic sensibilities."

This mission statement reflects the values of those who contributed to it. It is interesting to note that it makes no mention of the use of standardized tests to measure the achievement of the overarching goals.

To accomplish a school's mission, everyone working in the school must know the interrelationships among all components of the school and all employees and volunteers who work in the school. The principal's role is to work with teachers, parents, students, and community members to achieve some consensus concerning the school's mission and priorities, to unite everyone in and around the school to achieve the mission, and to orchestrate resources accordingly. This is the essence of a *shared vision* (Senge, 1990), a powerful tool because it involves and inspires each person on the team. Unfortunately, too many times an organization's vision is that of one person, the boss. We address the development of a shared vision in Chapter 4.

The New Rochelle mission statement quoted above does have shortcomings. For instance, it is implicit in the statement that schools exist solely for students. As we noted in Chapter 1, teachers must be treated as leaders and equals if they are to provide creative and dynamic learning environments for students. A fundamental tenet of TQE is that school districts are responsible for ensuring that work environments are provided in which teachers can achieve their number-one goal, helping young people learn.

Demonstrating Appreciation for a System

Demonstrating appreciation for a system by practicing it in the school is far more powerful than talking about it. Exhibit 2.1 provides a checklist that is useful for testing the degree to which appreciation for a system is infused in a school. In short, a system cannot be optimized without everyone's commitment to quality.

Knowledge of Variation

Knowledge of variation is really rather simple, but the mistakes that result when it is not understood can have severe consequences. Deming claims that two mistakes are frequently made:

1. *Treating an occurrence as if it came from a special cause of variation when it came from a common cause:* When schools fail to achieve their objectives, are the teachers at fault? Unless the precautions presented in Chapter 4 have been taken, they are likely not at fault. The cause is a common cause; the system is faulty, but teachers are often blamed. As Deming says, 85% of problems in an organization are the fault of the systems in place; only 15% are the fault of the people.

2. *Treating an occurrence as if it came from a common cause of variation when it came from a special cause:* An example of this would be failure to realize that a teacher's superior instruction occurred as a result of training the teacher received, and assuming instead that it occurred because improved performance was mandated.

The goal is to reduce both kinds of mistakes. Doing so results in a stable system, in which variation is predictable—that is, in which we can predict the outcomes of actions. The alternative is an unstable system, where results are so varied that prediction is not possible. When this is the case, we essentially have no idea what may happen next.

Teachers, like students, vary—no two are exactly alike. On any given test, approximately half will be above average and the other

Checklist for Assessing a School as a System

__ A high-quality mission has been developed with stake-holder involvement, adopted by all, and communicated to all.

__ Everyone in the organization is able to communicate the mission and his or her role in it.

__ Everyone communicates that the first focus is on quality—none does a mediocre job and passes on a faulty product to fellow workers.

__ Everyone knows the roles and structure of all components of the school.

__ Everyone actively helps others to do the very best job possible, and does not hesitate to seek assistance for him- or herself or peers.

__ Everyone demonstrates his or her understanding that an important avenue to maximum satisfaction in the long run is to work in a collegial work setting.

Exhibit 2.1.

half will be below average. This is like a blinding flash of the obvious. The salient question here is, How authentic is the measurement? What does it measure? Decisions made from bad data cannot be good decisions. (For a complete lesson in variation and its application to schools, see Latta & Downey, 1994.) Exhibit 2.2 contains a checklist that can be used to determine if a school is using knowledge of variation.

Theory of Knowledge

There are five important points to remember regarding the theory of knowledge:

- Information is not knowledge.

Checklist for Determining
Use of Knowledge of Variation

__ Everyone has been trained in the collection and use of data for improving systems.

__ Everyone uses appropriate data to make system decisions.

__ No one confuses common causes and special causes.

Exhibit 2.2.

- Management and leadership functions are predictions.
- Prediction (decision making) should be based on knowledge/theory.
- All rational decisions require prediction.
- We constantly make predictions.

Knowledge is theory that can be used reliably over time to make predictions; thus we use our knowledge/theory to make predictions. When a prediction is correct, the theory is strengthened. When it is wrong, the theory is, or should be, disproved or revised. Strong theory is built through systematic observation and revision. In folklore, the barnyard rooster Chanticleer formed a theory that aggrandized his status in life. He observed that the sun rose every morning after he crowed and flapped his wings, so he surmised that the sunrise was a result of his actions. However, one morning he overslept and did not crow, and the sun still came up. Ego deflated, he had to revise his theory.

Chanticleer saw information as knowledge. He used it as theory, a basis for prediction. Knowledge comes from theory. It endures over time and under a variety of circumstances. Theory allows us to predict outcomes. Prediction must be based on theory, not on casual observations untested under varying conditions. Had Chanticleer tested his theory, he would have revised it, even though the revision would not have served his ego so nicely. Deming (1992) offers another illustration of the difference between information and knowledge: "A dictionary contains information, but not knowledge. A dictionary is useful. I use a dictionary frequently when at my desk, but the dictionary will not prepare this paragraph nor criticize it" (p. 70). Mythological roosters are not alone in their failure to try out their ideas before proclaiming them as truth. In ancient Greece, Aristotle proclaimed that flies had five legs. People believed it; no one bothered to check. The advent of empiricism, of people seeking evidence in their environment, debunked the proclamation.

So what is the application of the theory of knowledge? One example can be found in a situation in which a few administrators and teachers attend a conference and learn a new teaching technique to which they respond very positively. In their exuberance, they assume all teachers will respond in the same way and value the technique also. The administrators mandate that all teachers over whom they have authority will experience training in the technique. Further, all teachers will be required to use the technique in their classrooms. In such an instance, the initial exuberance of those mandating the use of the technique might have sprung from the conference setting, the cleverness and humor of the instructor, or other factors irrelevant to the school setting. Whatever the reason, their experience may have been unique and ultimately irrelevant to their and their colleagues' actual teaching. It is not unusual for people to form assumptions in this manner; something like this has probably happened to all of us. The theory, that the new technique would apply in all teaching situations, was assumed before it was tested. Generalizations were made based on a limited number of experiences and perceptions and then applied without verification. Exhibit 2.3 provides a checklist that can be used to determine whether or not the theory of knowledge is being applied effectively at a school.

Knowledge of Psychology

Knowledge of psychology is crucial to educators. We do not have to be psychologists, but, as Deming emphasizes, we must know the fundamentals that will help us understand people and how they interact. For educators and other service professionals, the most profound knowledge we can gain from psychology includes two facts: (a) No two people are alike, and (b) intrinsic motivations

Checklist for Assessing the Use of Theory of
Knowledge

__ Teachers and administrators articulate their theories and how they use those theories in decision making.

__ Teachers and administrators try out their knowledge and theories to determine if they will stand the test of time.

__ Teachers and administrators do not use information as knowledge.

__ Teachers and administrators realize that knowledge and better practice come from theory.

__ Teachers and administrators understand that all decisions are based on theory.

Exhibit 2.3.

are far more powerful and have benefits far more long-lasting than do extrinsic motivations.

Our system of rewards in schools serves as an example of over-justification and could be improved by focusing on both intrinsic and extrinsic rewards. We observe that people feel good or appear relieved when they receive their paychecks, and we interpret that to mean that pay causes good morale and good work. We have no studies to prove this, but school boards, administrators, and teacher union leaders often insist that only money (higher salaries) be used to satisfy teachers and motivate them to do better work. In fact, the evidence that doing good work is a greater motivator than money is becoming overwhelming. Teachers should be compensated fairly because money is important. It fulfills some of life's basic needs, but it may not be the central motivator at work. However, it may be necessary to fulfill financial and security needs before needs for growth and self-actualization can be focused on by many employees (Frase, 1989; Herzberg, Mausner, & Snyderman, 1959).

The same is true for grades. We see smiles when students receive high grades, and we interpret that to mean that the grades are their reason for coming to school. They are not. Grades are imposed proxies for learning, just as a high salary is a proxy for good work. To test this theory, give only higher salaries to teachers or principals already making reasonable salaries and more A's to students and see if more and higher-quality work results. These tactics may bring smiles, but their effects will be short-lived. Humans do things for intrinsic reasons, reasons that are far more powerful than extrinsic rewards. We do not need proxies for good work and learning; both are powerful rewards in and of themselves. Exhibit 2.4 provides a checklist that can be used to assess a school's status regarding knowledge of psychology.

The final four areas of profound knowledge to be discussed are flow, autotelic jobs, abundance and scarcity mentality, and efficacy and locus of control. Just as the four original TQE areas of profound knowledge are totally interdependent, so are these added areas.

Flow, the Optimal Experience

We experience flow when we are immersed in a task for the joy of doing it, just as learners do (see English & Hill, 1994). By building understanding of flow and its elements into a job, we can help teachers achieve this state in their jobs. We have all had times when we felt in control of our lives, instead of feeling as though we were being buffeted by external forces. On these rare occasions we feel a sense of exhilaration, a deep sense of enjoyment that is long cherished and that becomes a benchmark in memory for what life should be like (Csikszentmihalyi, 1990). This is flow, the ultimate experience, as Tzu described *Yu*. People report experiencing flow as they take part in many recreational activities, such as gardening, exercise, and fishing. They also report experiencing it in their work. We ourselves have experienced flow in teaching, administrating, and writing.

Autotelic Jobs

The word *autotelic* is formed from two Greek words: *auto*, meaning "self," and *telos*, meaning "goal." Thus an autotelic job is one in which

---

Checklist for Assessing the Use of
Knowledge of Psychology

In this school, teachers and administrators focus on:

__ the rich rewards that come from helping young people
learn

__ the pleasure teachers can experience when their instructional abilities are enhanced through professional
growth and development

__ learning, as demonstrated by students' expressions of joy
in learning, not progress quotas and subjective ratings

__ the degree to which teachers demonstrate joy in their
work as a barometer of organizational health

__ the search for ways to improve the work environment
(processes, procedures, conditions) to enable teachers to
help young people learn

Exhibit 2.4.

the worker finds an inextricable, intrinsic motivation in the job
itself. Research from around the world has shown that jobs yielding
flow, as described above, have four conditions in common:

- Variety
- Appropriate and flexible challenges
- Clear goals
- Immediate feedback (Csikszentmihalyi, 1990, p. 154)

These conditions have been found in jobs that require advanced
skills or little skill, filled by people representing all income levels
and walks of life.

In reading our description of flow in the first paragraph of this
chapter, some readers may have dismissed it as pretty airy-fairy
stuff. After all, flowing, or walking without one's feet touching the
ground, does sound a bit strange. Descriptions of flow may initially sound strange and out of touch with reality, but the four
common conditions of autotelic jobs bring flow into real-life per-

Checklist for Assessing the Application of Autotelic Jobs

__ Care is taken to redesign teachers' jobs to ensure greater satisfaction. Adequate variety exists in the job; teachers do not simply teach the same one or two courses all day long.

__ The improvement ethic is in place. Teachers are consulted regarding their professional growth. Appropriate provisions are made for continued career development.

__ Clear goals exist for the day, week, and year; teachers are not just told to "do the best they can."

__ The principal models the improvement ethic by continually learning, trying out ideas, assessing benefits, and trying again.

__ The principal actively seeks and accepts constructive criticism as a means of doing superior work.

__ The principal gives specific feedback to teachers on instruction and interpersonal relations.

Exhibit 2.5.

spective. These are elements most people want in their work, according to research in industry and education (Hackman & Oldham, 1980; Harder, 1985; Spangler, 1985).

In creating autotelic jobs in teaching, the role of leaders is to entreat every teacher to look forward and inward, to discover his or her own internal standards. Exhibit 2.5 is a checklist that can be used to determine the degree to which administrative behavior ensures that teaching is an autotelic job, or one that results in flow.

Abundance and Scarcity Mentality

Principals who honestly share recognition and power are practicing from an abundance mentality. The rationale is simple: Neither recognition nor power is in limited supply. Some teachers seem relectant to share their personal discoveries about teaching and teaching techniques with other teachers. Some principals seldom give honest compliments. On some level, such people believe that giving to others means there will be less for them, that one person's success requires another person's failure. This has been termed *mutually exclusive goal attainment* (MEGA) (Kohn, 1986) and the *scarcity mentality* (Covey, 1991). In truth, there is no scarcity. In fact, the more we give away, the greater the return to us. The abundance mentality leads to helping, sharing, complimenting, and giving recognition. Working from an abundance mentality fosters growth, self-respect, feelings of self-worth, appreciation, recognition, and a benevolent desire for mutual respect for the giver and the receiver. The scarcity mentality reduces all of these. The checklist in Exhibit 2.6 can help teachers and administrators identify which mentality pervades their schools.

Efficacy and Locus of Control

Having a high sense of efficacy means that one believes one can make things happen or keep them from happening. We know that a high sense of teacher efficacy is strongly related to student achievement (Ashton & Webb, 1986). People with internal locus of control believe they can control some things in their lives. We know that internal locus of control is highly related to individual and personal achievement. This holds true for teachers and administrators, those at the center of school improvement.

School principals are charged with the responsibility of orchestrating the many components of a school to achieve goals. Unsuccessful principals tell us that they are not in control of their days, let alone their schools and the schools' futures. They say that strong external forces are at work, changing the direction of their schools. In sharp contrast, principals characterized by internal locus of control tend to be successful. They have "can-do" attitudes; they are in charge. School leaders must govern their own futures and those of their schools; they cannot leave leadership to powerful external forces. They must work with everyone in their schools to shift the locus of control from one of "poor me" helplessness to a can-do attitude. With others, school leaders must establish goals and the means for attaining them, monitor progress, and

Checklist for Determining the
Use of the Abundance Mentality

___ Specific compliments are given frequently.

___ Advice and assistance are given freely to others to help them improve.

___ There is a sense of joy and higher self-esteem in helping others.

___ Recognition is given for the accomplishments of fellow teachers, administrators, students, and parents.

Exhibit 2.6.

redirect their organizations as necessary. School staff must be in charge of schools and responsible for them. Schools must have strong organizational efficacy and internal locus of control. Exhibit 2.7 provides a checklist that can be used to measure the extent to which a school has high organizational efficacy and internal locus of control.

The Challenge

Using profound knowledge is the essence of the challenge—to optimize schools, to create school environments where teachers can teach and students can learn. So what's new? Good question. Using profound knowledge is new. It is not mystical. Successes gained through the proper application of profound knowledge through TQE have been demonstrated in schools and industry. The profound knowledge areas we have discussed in this chapter are applying systems theory; using knowledge of variation, theories of knowledge, and knowledge of psychology; understanding flow as an optimal experience; providing conditions where teaching can be an autotelic job; practicing the abundance mentality and eschewing the scarcity mentality; and building efficacy and internal locus of control for every individual.

Checklist for Assessing Organizational Locus
of Control and Efficacy

___ Problems are viewed as challenges.

___ Administrators and teachers take responsibility for what happens at the school, both the good and the bad.

___ Administrators and teachers demonstrate a can-do spirit.

___ Administrators and teachers plan and take charge of what happens at the school.

___ Administrators and teachers find that someone or something keeps imposing rules and changes on the school.

___ Administrators and teachers find it impossible to catch up.

Exhibit 2.7.

Inherent in profound knowledge is the TQE belief that the focus must be on improving the system, not on judging short- or long-term performances or gains. When we wait until the end of the year to judge student achievement with tests, we may be measuring the wrong criteria, and, further, we have no chance to make adjustments. Judging teachers' performance annually and giving them ratings is subject to the same criticism. As teachers, principals, and superintendents, we cannot be with all students or all teachers at the same time. To judge anyone for a full year based on a snapshot analysis is foolhardy, removes a very powerful internal motivator, and makes people dependent on external motivators—ratings. Instead, the teacher's job should be to focus on student learning, ensuring that it is pleasurable. Administrators must view the employees in their buildings as internal customers and ensure that conditions are present in which teachers, custodians, and teacher aides can experience pride and success in their work, where they can learn and develop into even better teachers, custodians, and aides. When joy and pride in learning and teaching are experienced, when learners and teachers are independent and accountable to themselves, all else will follow, for, as Ralph Waldo Emerson has noted, "The joy of a thing well done is to have done it."

Key Terms and Concepts

Abundance mentality. Mentality stemming from the belief that there is no scarcity of potential success, which leads to the conclusion that by helping others to achieve success one can attain success oneself.

Autotelic job. Work characterized by variety, flexible challenges, clear goals, and immediate feedback (*autotelic* is from the Greek words *auto* [self] and *telos* [goal]).

Chanticleer. The mythological rooster who believed his crowing caused the sun to rise each morning.

Common cause. A cause of variation that is generally the fault of problems in the system that can be controlled by the system.

Flow. The state of being immersed in a task for the joy of doing it; similar to *Yu* and *ikigai.*

Ikigai. Japanese word describing "that which makes life worth living."

Locus of control. A personality variable concerning the place where control is perceived to originate. Internal locus of control describes people who believe they can, to a large extent, control their future and do not have to leave it to the fates, powerful others, and other external factors; external locus of control describes people who believe they cannot control their futures and thus must leave them to the fates and external powers.

Mutually exclusive goal attainment (MEGA). Similar to scarcity mentality, this describes situations in which people behave as though the only way for them to succeed is by preventing others from succeeding.

Optimal experience. Being in the state of flow referred to as *Yu* and *ikigai.*

Optimization. The state when maximum productivity and improvement are achieved, when all systems and procedures work together to accomplish an organization's or individual's mission.

Organizational efficacy. The belief on the part of organization members that if they do certain things they can achieve organizational success.

Profound knowledge. The knowledge that provides a lens, or map, of theory for understanding and optimizing organizations.

Scarcity mentality. Mentality stemming from the belief that potential success is scarce and therefore the way to succeed is to prevent others from succeeding; similar to MEGA.

Shared vision. A goal or mission that unites every person in an organization.

Special causes. Those causes of variation that are not part of the system of common causes, beyond the control of the system.

Suboptimized. The state of an organization or person when productivity and improvement are lacking, when all systems and procedures are not working together to accomplish the organization's or individual's mission.

Yu. The word used by Taoist scholar Chuang Tzu as a synonym for the right way of following the path, the right way to live.

References

Ashton, P. T., & Webb, R. B. (1986). *Making a difference: Teacher sense of efficacy and student achievement.* New York: Longman.

Covey, S. R. (1991). *Principle-centered leadership.* New York: Summit.

Csikszentmihalyi, M. (1990). *Flow: The psychology of optimal experience.* New York: Harper Perennial.

Deming, W. E. (1992, October). *Quality, productivity, and competitive position.* Paper presented at the Quality Enhancement Seminars, Los Angeles.

English, F. W., & Hill, J. C. (1994). *Total quality education: Transforming schools into learning places.* Thousand Oaks, CA: Corwin.

Frase, L. E. (1989). The effects of teaching rewards on recognition and job enrichment. *Journal of Educational Research, 83*(1), 53-57.

Hackman, J., & Oldham, G. (1980). *Work redesign.* Menlo Park, CA: Addison-Wesley.

Harder, W. W. (1985). *Teacher job satisfaction: An application and expansion of the job characteristics model of work motivation.* Unpublished doctoral dissertation, University of Wisconsin–Milwaukee.

Herzberg, F., Mausner, B., & Snyderman, B. (1959). *The motivation to work.* New York: John Wiley.

Kohn, A. (1986). *No contest.* Boston: Houghton Mifflin.

Latta, R., & Downey, C. J. (1994). *Tools for achieving TQE.* Thousand Oaks, CA: Corwin.

Sarason, S. B. (1990). *The predictable failure of school reform.* San Francisco: Jossey-Bass.

Senge, P. M. (1990). *The fifth discipline: The art and practice of the learning organization.* New York: Doubleday/Currency.

Spangler, W. D. (1985). *The validity of the job characteristics model.* Unpublished doctoral dissertation, University of Michigan.

✦ 3 ✦

Achieving the Transformation:
Teachers' Role
in School Management

School Reform and Teacher Involvement

We suggested earlier that ensuring that TQE does not become simply a transitory phenomenon in schools involves developing it with the intent of fostering a genuinely participatory or "organic" approach to management at the school level. In this spirit, the goals of TQE are to promote closer working relationships among teachers, administrators, and students, and to facilitate teacher involvement. Only then can TQE represent a significant shift in the way schools are managed. As a corporate executive recently stated to one of us, "If four or five teachers in a school can't come into the principal's office and say, 'We've got a problem with something in this school,' you don't have [TQE]."

Indeed, Deming's ideas regarding employee involvement have much relevance to the present educational reform movement. This reform movement has progressed in two distinct phases. The first began in the early 1980s and featured reform proposals formulated by state-level public officials, with relatively little input from teachers. These initial measures, such as merit pay and teacher competency tests, implicitly suggested that greater bureaucratic regulation of teachers' work would lead to school improvement. The second phase of the reform movement was characterized by recommendations developed largely in reaction to the bureaucratic tendencies of the early measures. Reports from the Carnegie Forum on Education and the Economy (1986) and the Holmes Group (1986) encouraged the development of a framework for collegial and participative decision making at the school level. The Carnegie Forum, for example, maintains that "school systems based on bureaucratic authority must be replaced by schools in which authority is grounded in the professional competence of the teacher [and] where teachers work together as colleagues" (p. 55).

During the second phase of reform, many school districts experimented with site-based management, career ladders, and innovative labor relations approaches. These various efforts shared the intent of increasing teacher involvement in the decision-making process in schools. The question emerges, however, as to whether these experiments will permanently change the way that school systems in this country are managed. The answer to that question is likely to hinge on how well reform-minded teachers and managers are able to reinvent managerial processes in their schools that more fully bring teachers into the decision-making process in schools.

Myths and Realities: The Quiet Compromise in School Management and Leadership

Cooper (1991) points out that two central myths guide the thinking of both teachers and administrators about how schools are and ought to be managed. One myth supports the theory that schools are run by those nominally in charge: boards of education, superintendents, assistants, and other top-level bureaucrats. The central office sets the direction for the schools; rules and directives come from the top, and teachers, as subordinates, follow. The opposite myth also exists: that schools are actually managed by those closest to the students and the teaching-learning process—the teachers, department chairs, and others who work with students.

The result is a "quiet compromise" between teachers and administrators, whereby:

> teachers nod at top-down directives, while closing their classroom doors and doing mainly what they choose. Superintendents and staff hold meetings, promulgate policies, and set procedures, but much of what the central office mandates is irrelevant to teachers and can easily be overlooked. . . . [E]ach group holds the belief that they have the final word, while giving lip service to the other. (Cooper, 1991, p. 260)

However, neither myth is based in an accurate depiction of schools. Although administrators may prefer to think of themselves and school boards as possessing authority over the key policy and management decisions in schools, it is teachers who decide which policy directives will actually be implemented. And although teachers have classroom autonomy, it is administrators who decide many of the key issues affecting teachers in their individual classrooms, such as how students will be assigned to classes, how teachers will be assigned to classes, and how students will be disciplined and promoted.

But because many teachers and administrators firmly believe their respective myths, a quiet compromise results, making many school organizations excessively rigid and incapable of change. Instead, observers argue, a new organizational form is needed, a "participative management" approach, whereby central school boards devolve authority to schools, and principals in turn share decision-making power with teachers. By involving teachers in setting school and district goals and priorities, distributing resources, and shaping programs, empowerment "permeates the system from top to bottom" (Cooper, 1991, p. 268).

However, the managerial systems of many schools fail to provide mechanisms by which administrators, teachers, and parents can jointly identify and solve problems and mobilize resources. To the degree that a quiet compromise is struck between teachers and administrators, teachers cannot easily bring problems to the attention of administrators or engage them in dialogue about resource allocation. Perhaps part of the discomfort experienced by teachers in their interactions with management stems from competing values and models held by administrators and professionals.

Bureaucratic Versus Professional Models of School Management

Most discussions of school management implicitly focus on the differences between two models, one bureaucratic and the other professional. The bureaucratic model emphasizes clear lines of authority and rules formulated by superiors to govern the behavior of subordinates. The professional model, in contrast, stresses multidirectional patterns of communication and power, as well as the achievement of coordination through employee commitment rather than through top-down controls (Bacharach & Conley, 1986).

The contrasting features of these models point to a pivotal tension in school management between the concepts of control and autonomy. The bureaucratic model is often interpreted as suggesting that the manager's job is to control teachers through specifying their work procedures in detail. The professional model is interpreted as implying freedom from these controls.

However, both models, the bureaucratic and the professional, in fact address important needs in school management. The professional model suggests that teachers must have discretion in the classroom to address the diverse and constantly changing needs of students. That is, the model underscores that teachers require discretion to make decisions under conditions of inherent classroom uncertainty and unpredictability. The bureaucratic model suggests that the efforts of individual teachers (who are collectively responsible for educating students over 12 years) must be coordinated (Bacharach & Conley, 1986).

At first, these two models of school management seem contradictory. How can teachers be controlled but still given substantial freedom? However, the models can be complementary. The key is, How can the efforts of autonomous teachers ultimately achieve some coordination and overall integration of effort?

TQE can be viewed as one means for reaching an appropriate compromise between the extremes of teacher autonomy and managerial control. On one hand, several of Deming's 14 points stress the importance of coordination of individual efforts; for example, Deming emphasizes that barriers between departments must be broken down (Point 9). On the other hand, Deming states that individual employee initiative and creativity are critical, stressing that managers should drive out fear (Point 8) and cease the need for constant inspection that stifles initiative (Point 3). Thus Deming emphasizes both organization coordination and individual discretion. Both requirements are important: One critical element of school management should not be pursued at the expense of the other. In the next section we provide more details on how to begin bridging the gap between bureaucracy and professionalism.

Administering Through TQE: Guidelines for School Management

Marshall (1992) uses the metaphor of a wide chasm to describe the differing perspectives of teachers and administrators. On one side of the chasm are teachers, who embody professional autonomy, and on the other side are administrators, who embody managerial control. The following guidelines may be helpful for bridging the worlds of teachers and administrators by encouraging a sense of purpose that also allows for teacher initiative, leadership, and participation in school management:

1. Reevaluate the roles of teachers, principals, and higher-level administrators.
2. Enhance teacher commitment and self-esteem.
3. Provide teachers with opportunities to attain greater levels of intrinsic and extrinsic rewards.
4. Exhibit positive supervision in schools.
5. Provide teachers with a sense of professionalism and career growth.

6. Encourage teacher collaboration and teamwork.
7. Enhance teacher participation in school decision making.
8. Promote a culture of shared values.

Explanations of these guidelines are provided below.

Reevaluate the roles of teachers, principals, and higher-level administrators. The reinvention of school management with an eye toward a participatory approach requires a reevaluation of the respective roles of teachers, principals, and district administrators. The traditional view of teachers is that they are subordinates in an organizational hierarchy, and as such carry out expert decisions organized and planned by others at higher organizational levels. A quality management orientation implies that organizational knowledge rests with teachers; thus they must have considerable latitude in planning and executing work decisions. From this perspective, teachers are the "line decision makers" for the organization because they are literally on the line with clients (i.e., students), handling uncertainty for the organization (Conley & Bacharach, 1990). Because teachers manage uncertainty, their activities cannot be delineated by those outside of the classroom. As the members of school systems with the most intimate knowledge of customer needs, teachers are in a position to identify resource requirements for principals.

The traditional conception of principals is that they are managers who inspect and control the work of teachers. TQE principals facilitate the work of teachers by encouraging teachers to identify their resource needs, by fulfilling those needs, and, when necessary, by communicating teacher needs to higher levels of administration. Indeed, principals are often characterized as "middle managers" caught between the demands of teacher professionals in buildings and the demands of superiors in the administrative hierarchy. A TQE-inspired approach, however, casts principals not only as managers but also as instructional leaders. As instructional leaders, principals are the visible spokespersons of schools who express and embody the schools' purposes and encourage reflection about how daily activities are related to those purposes. Principals are critical for shaping a positive school culture, because they visibly articulate the educational values of parents, teachers, students, and community members (see Willower, 1984).

The traditional view of district administrators is that they function as the repository of organizational knowledge (which is then carried down the hierarchy) as well as the guardian of educational standards. A TQE-oriented approach characterizes district-level administrators not as guardians but as facilitators of standards. Deming's "downstream" leadership notion (see Chapter 1) implies that district-level administrators are charged with providing general policy direction and allocating resources to schools. School principals and teachers are then viewed more as the clients of central administrators than simply as employees to be monitored and supervised. Under this conception, central administrators' responsiveness to principals builds a domino effect, whereby principals become responsive to teachers and teachers to their students. In sum, TQE requires that the respective roles of teachers, building administrators, and district administrators be identified and clarified for all organizational participants.

Enhance teacher commitment and self-esteem. Bureaucratic management practices of the past involve the formulation of rules by top-level administrators to govern the behavior of subordinate teachers. In both the public and the private sectors there has been an increasing acceptance of the doctrine, consistent with TQE, that one can elicit employee commitment by relying on employees to design their own methods for pursuing collective objectives, as opposed to using top-down management controls to govern employee behavior. Contemporary management techniques, then, seek to foster commitment instead of control over teachers' work activities.

Teacher commitment and self-esteem are maximized when managers treat teachers as professionals in the workplace. To achieve this goal, managers must do the following:

- Show respect for teachers' professional judgment and initiative by encouraging creative risk taking and tolerating failure.

- Respect teachers' professional initiative as exercised in their separate classrooms, as well as the collective judgments of teachers.
- Provide teachers with opportunities to participate in schoolwide decision making, through such roles as committee members, chairs or cochairs of site councils, and members of interdisciplinary teams, and see that the decisions teachers make receive resource support.
- Delegate significant as opposed to trivial decisions to teacher teams, such as student and teacher scheduling, program and budget development, grading and promotion policies, and facilities management.

Provide teachers with opportunities to attain greater levels of intrinsic and extrinsic rewards. Teachers entering the profession place high value on the intrinsic or "psychic" rewards that come from reaching students and helping them learn (Lortie, 1975). Within the context of the ideals of TQE, teachers come into the profession highly motivated to focus on quality. However, if schools do not provide work environments where teachers can realize their intrinsic motivations, they may become dissatisfied and eventually leave the profession.

Although intrinsic rewards are paramount in teaching, extrinsic features of work, such as salary, supervision, and advancement, should not be discounted. Teachers have reasonable expectations regarding their levels of pay, and are concerned, particularly early in their careers, with economic security for themselves and, for many, their families.

Numerous schools, however, as they are currently structured, do not provide teachers with high levels of intrinsic and extrinsic rewards. Indeed, many of the early reform proposals, such as merit pay, were based on assumptions that teachers were instrumentally oriented to their work (i.e., motivated by financial gain) and neglected the intrinsic dimensions of teachers' work. The second wave of reforms, which focused on teacher professionalism, redirected attention to intrinsic work factors, including work autonomy, opportunities for personal growth and development, and chances to use complex skills.

In this spirit, school managers who are interested in promoting teachers' intrinsic rewards might consider implementing the following:

- Work redesign strategies based on detailed analyses of teachers' work characteristics (see Chapter 5)
- Career development systems or career lattices aimed toward providing teachers with greater opportunities for skill development and career growth in the profession of teaching
- Strategies that provide individual teachers and groups of teachers (e.g., teachers on multilevel age or interdisciplinary teams) significant discretion to set directions for their own work and monitor progress in such areas as curriculum development, pedagogical techniques, discipline policies, in-service training, and parent involvement strategies

Exhibit positive supervision in schools. Nowhere is the tension between bureaucratic and professional models of school management more apparent than in the context of teacher supervision. If school managers aim to provide teachers with greater involvement in day-to-day decision making, but then use bureaucratic techniques (e.g., "simple" checklists; see Chapter 4) in their evaluation and supervisory processes, they will have accomplished little.

Because many principals are keenly aware of the tension between bureaucratic structures and professional norms, they tend to avoid the supervision of teachers or to treat the process superficially. In one district in Washington, D.C. (discussed in greater depth in Chapter 4), about one-third of scheduled evaluations were not conducted (Frase & Streshly, 1994). Of those that were conducted, principals spent very little time in the teachers' classrooms and delivered very general or otherwise unhelpful reports to teachers. Perhaps many principals, in an effort to respect teachers' desires for discretion and to serve as judges of ther own work, decide to meet minimal district standards for observations, interceding only when the most obvious needs and problems arise. However, this strategy restricts the exchange of information between teachers and administrators and consequently the improvement of systems and work processes within the school. Managers who use positive supervisory practices respect the judgment and initiative of professional teachers at the same time they provide constructive suggestions and resource support.

The checklist in Exhibit 3.1 can be used by administrators to assess the degree to which teachers find administrators' suggestions for resource support to be helpful or unhelpful in providing instruction. The first four items in the exhibit indicate positive supervision; the last two denote negative supervision. We consider that 100% positive responses to the first four items and 100% negative responses to the last two items are necessary to indicate positive supervision. Administrators who do not believe they would obtain the proper responses to these items should consider means for changing their practices so that they can be of greater assistance to teachers in their work.

Provide teachers with a sense of professionalism and career growth. Teaching is often viewed as a "flat" occupation that provides teachers few opportunities for career growth and professional advancement. After all, many teachers who want to advance often do so either by moving into administration or by entering another profession. Even some teacher "career ladders" encourage the most highly qualified teachers to move out of the classroom and assume a variety of nonteaching duties. This strikes many observers as a curious way to upgrade the status of the teaching profession. Could career development strategies be designed instead to encourage and recognize greater and greater levels of teachers' professional skill and development? Such systems would have as their primary goal the development of teachers within the profession of teaching. They would also focus on providing all teachers—not a select few—with opportunities to grow and develop professionally.

Several teacher career development plans in the state of Arizona have strived to conform to these ideals. One district with which the second author has worked places emphasis on the development of pretenure teachers; movement onto the career ladder, and an accompanying salary increase, coincides with the granting of tenure. Career ladder teachers also participate in a variety of skill growth and professional development activities, such as

---

Checklist for Determining Helpfulness of Supervision

Would teachers in my school say:

__ "My principal or supervisor shows appreciation for my work and has confidence in me"? ___ yes ___ no

__ "My principal or supervisor explains things or gives information or suggestions"? ___ yes ___ no

__ "My principal or supervisor asks for my suggestions or opinions"? ___ yes ___ no

__ "My principal or supervisor asks for information, clarification, or explanation"? ___ yes ___ no

__ "My principal or supervisor criticizes me, refuses to help, or is unnecessarily formal"? ___ yes ___ no

__ "My principal or supervisor gives excess, unnecessary information or comments"? ___ yes ___ no

---

Exhibit 3.1.

(Adapted from Bacharach, Bauer, & Conley, 1986)

study teams, project teams, and peer assistance. These career development systems appear to be providing teachers with greater levels of intrinsic and extrinsic rewards in the teaching profession.

Encourage teacher collaboration and teamwork. Unfortunately, the current structure of schools makes it difficult for teachers to coordinate their separate efforts. Restrictive time schedules and norms of teacher isolation make it hard for teachers to share their wealth of knowledge, skills, and information. Further obstacles to coordination are the bureaucratic structure of school organizations and its accompanying compartmentalization of job responsibilities, which largely confine the teacher's role to that of a "technician" in the classroom. The definition of teaching as work that occurs only in classrooms contributes further to the isolation of teachers.

In schools that are particularly effective, teachers have opportunities to engage in constant dialogue and substantive exchange about how they teach. This information exchange provides a mechanism for coordinating teachers' separate efforts. Such coordination is particularly important in professional settings such as schools, where professionals are serving (or will serve) the same clients.

School managers who want to bring about greater coordination of teachers' work efforts might consider the following steps:

- Involve teachers in (or delegate to teachers) decisions about work schedules and preparation time.

- Help teachers free up time for the purpose of facilitating greater professional interaction. For example, administrators might discuss with teachers ideas for restructuring the school day, volunteer to take over classes for teachers, or locate people in the community who could be utilized for such purposes (e.g., fully qualified retired teachers).

- Form a teacher committee charged with developing creative solutions to problems of time. The committee's detailed recommendations could then be forwarded to the principal for approval and resource support.

Enhance teacher participation in school decision making. Although teachers are those most knowledgeable about the school's primary clients (the students), they are often unable to exchange information or expand the scope of their decision making. "Participation" as a managerial strategy serves to militate against the teacher's solitary role by ensuring the coordination of teachers' efforts in the school. Participatory mechanisms that are being adopted in schools include site-based management, middle school programs, and peer assistance programs.

Participation has both vertical and horizontal components. Teachers participate vertically when they influence decisions typically made by higher-level administrators. Teachers participate horizontally, in contrast, when they participate in decisions made by or for their fellow teachers. Although the literature generally confines the discussion of participation to vertical processes, most forms of participation are likely to have vertical and horizontal elements. For example, if a teacher and his or her principal agree on a work assignment that ultimately affects the work assignments and/or resources of other teachers, then the teacher's involvement

Questions for Administrators

1. Would teachers in your school say that they have significant input into the following decisions? (non-exhaustive list)

__ How to teach

__ What to teach

__ Scheduling students and teachers

__ Selecting instructional resources

__ Setting or revising disciplinary policies

__ School budget decisions

__ Decisions about the school facility

__ Decisions about staff hiring

__ Decisions about how teachers are evaluated

2. If your school has a school improvement team, site-based management council, or shared decision-making structure, does the school team or council

__ include representatives of all relevant stakeholders, such as administrators, teachers, parents, students, community members? ___ yes ___ no

__ have the authority to make decisions on substantive issues such as budget, personnel, and program? [1] ___ yes ___ no

__ provide stakeholders with an opportunity to determine or easily contribute items for the meeting agendas? ___ yes ___ no

3. If you were to hire an outside consultant to interview members of your team or council, how would team members respond to the following statements?

__ We feel perfectly comfortable adding controversial items to the meeting agenda. __ agree __ disagree

Exhibit 3.2.

__ We are confident that these items will receive a fair hearing in the council or team. ___ agree ___ disagree

__ Each team/council member is encouraged to share his or her viewpoints and perspectives at team/council meetings. ___ agree ___ disagree

__ The team/council has significant influence over important school management issues, such as personnel, program, and budget. ___ agree ___ disagree

__ Decisions reached by the team are acted upon, either by members of the team itself or by school management. ___ agree ___ disagree

4. An acid test for a decision-making group or team is whether decisions have been made and acted upon. To gauge your team or council's success, list the decisions implemented by your team or council during the past year:

If you did not cite any decisions, it is time to rethink the purpose and function of your team. If your team or council has implemented decisions, have these decisions been monitored to determine whether they accomplished the intent of the school improvement effort? The team can use such information to improve (constantly and forever) systems within the school that will allow principals, teachers, and students to perform to their maximum potential.

---

1. This question was inspired by Malen and Ogawa's (1988) finding that school advisory councils rarely featured teachers and parent participation in significant decisions related to budget, personnel, and program.

Exhibit 3.2. Continued

is both horizontal and vertical. To use another illustration, a peer assistance team that influences a principal's decision concerning the tenure of a probationary teacher exercises vertical and horizontal participation as well. Thus participation strategies intended to be vertical may have horizontal effects.

Managers who are interested in assuring teachers greater horizontal and vertical participation in school decision-making processes can select from a variety of reforms that appear to enhance teacher involvement. Exhibit 3.2 lists some questions that administrators might consider.

Promote a culture of shared values. A positive school culture is one in which parents, students, teachers, and community members share important values about the education of children. In this context, the school principal is a cultural leader who helps build ties between the community and the school to enhance community and teacher involvement. The checklist in Exhibit 3.3 might be used by principals to help determine the degree to which they and their schools are involving the community and promoting a positive school culture.

In this context, an important contribution of a community-oriented TQE process is that it helps schools meet the demands of rapidly changing community and social contexts by making the organization reflective of community values and capable of continuous change and improvement.

The Match Between TQE and Multiple Frameworks of Organizations

Multiple analytic paradigms and approaches can give a more complete picture of how TQM might work in an organization. Morgan (1986), for example, explains that organizations include "complex and paradoxical phenomena that can be understood in many different ways" (p. 13). He urges managers to utilize different images or metaphors in understanding organizations, such as the organization as machine, the organization as brain, or the organization as culture. Similarly, Bolman and Deal (1993) suggest that "the

Checklist on Community Involvement

__ There is a system in place for determining community preferences.

__ School administrators and faculty have worked with community groups to build support.

__ School administrators and faculty have shared the school's mission and plans for improvement with local citizens.

__ School administrators and faculty have established programs or events devoted to academics that have become school and community traditions.

__ School administrators and faculty have set goals that appeal to the values of community groups and have demonstrated how specific programs and daily decisions are related to general values.

__ School administrators and faculty have appealed to the values of diverse interest groups through the goal-setting process of the school.

Exhibit 3.3.
(Adapted from Willower, 1984)

inability to consider *multiple* perspectives continually undermines efforts to manage or change organizations" (p. 309; emphasis added). Different organizational frameworks can be viewed as "shorthand ways of describing the perspectives of different students and practitioners as to 'how things work' " (Scull & Conley, in press).

Managers should become aware of four frameworks that have guided the development of organizational theory: structural, human relations, political, and symbolic (Bolman & Deal, 1993). The *structural* frame assumes that organizations exist primarily to accomplish goals, such as efficiency and productivity. It further assumes that in any organization, it is possible for managers to design an appropriate structure to maximize the organization's goals. The *human relations* frame asserts that organizations exist primarily to serve human needs, and that both people and the organization benefit when these needs are satisfied in the workplace. The *political* frame assumes that organizations are coalitions of different individuals and groups who have different values, beliefs, resources, and perceptions of reality. Conflict between individuals and groups is thus inherent to organizational life, and this conflict produces organizational "winners" and "losers." The *symbolic* frame assumes that events and processes in organizations are inherently ambiguous and uncertain. In the context of uncertainty and ambiguity, organizational participants create symbols (e.g., myths and rituals) to reduce uncertainty and provide direction. Symbols also help the organization to acquire the support and faith of clients, patrons, and experts outside of the organization that are necessary for the organization's survival.

The principles of Total Quality Management draw most heavily from structural and human relations views of organizations; that is, their scope is limited largely to structural influences and human concerns. Structural influences can be seen in Deming's emphasis on such things as planning, staying focused on goals, improving work processes, reducing variation, and improving employee training. The tenets of human relations-oriented theory can be seen in Deming's notion that if the system is designed correctly, managers will be less inclined to violate human needs by focusing on end-of-the-line inspection or "managing by fear." Management by fear is counterproductive. Managerial strategies aimed at driving out fear include ceasing the need for inspection, enhancing employee teamwork, and increasing pride in workmanship. Both the people and the organization win when the organization's structures and processes are optimally designed. The people win because they can work in a nonthreatening atmosphere that fosters pride and teamwork, and the organization wins because optimal design results in increased worker productivity and efficiency.

A notable human relations-inspired application of TQM in education, or TQE, is that advanced by Seymour Sarason (1993), who suggests that the school work environment must be responsive to the needs of teachers and students. Principles that would be featured in such a work environment include the following (Forester, 1991, cited in Sarason, 1993):

- End the practice of dwelling on the cost of quality education and look instead for effective ways of fostering learning.
- Build a collaborative environment where teachers work together to make decisions and solve issues that have direct relevance to their and their students' lives.
- Reduce the dependence on tests and examinations to achieve quality and instead build ongoing feedback and evaluation among teachers, students, and staff in order to improve quality.
- Recognize that quality control and accountability are not simply the responsibility of managers but occur horizontally and vertically in educational organizations, because teachers and principals are colleagues, not merely subordinates and superiors.

To the degree that school administrators are wedded to a particular view of organizations, they are likely to view TQE in different ways. Structural managers, for example, would be likely to adopt an administrative perspective, viewing TQE as a structural change necessary to increase organizational productivity. A human relations manager might caution that TQE-oriented change prescriptions must achieve a "fit" with the needs of teachers in his or her particular school. A political manager who is sensitive to the balance of power between teachers and administrators might caution that TQE should increase the power of teachers to influence management's decisions, and not the other way around. Finally, to a symbolic manager, TQE may represent a ritual for producing symbols and negotiating new meanings within a school. TQE may also serve as a signal to outsiders (e.g., parents, community) that the school is accountable and responsive to clients.

A "multiframework" approach, then, sensitizes managers to the complex and sometimes paradoxical nature of organizations. Managers who can draw from a multiframework view of organizations are likely to give careful and judicious attention to the multifaceted consequences of any change attempt. TQE, like any change effort, will require new structural alignments in the organization, will affect human needs and concerns, will cause conflict between potential "winners" and "losers," and will result in new symbols, myths, and meanings for organizational participants. Managers drawing upon a multiframework view would proceed with TQE-oriented changes cautiously, taking into consideration these various frameworks and worldviews.

Key Terms and Concepts

Extrinsic rewards. Work-related rewards that derive from such features of work as pay, opportunities for advancement, supervision, and relationships with coworkers.

Horizontal participation. Teacher involvement in decision making that affects peers or fellow teachers.

Intrinsic rewards. Work-related rewards that derive from aspects of the work itself, including job challenge, autonomy, a chance to use one's own special abilities, and feedback from the job itself.

Teacher career ladders. One popular form of teacher work redesign that normally focuses on providing teachers with opportunities for enhanced professional growth and career advancement.

Teacher work redesign. A strategy that relates salary to redefined work roles and extended work schedules (definition adopted from Malen, Murphy, & Hart, 1987, p. 119).

Vertical participation. Teacher involvement in decision making that affects higher-level administrators.

References

Bacharach, S. B., Bauer, S. C., & Conley, S. C. (1986). Organizational analysis of stress: The case of elementary and secondary schools. *Sociology of Work and Occupations, 13,* 7-32.

Bacharach, S. B., & Conley, S. C. (1986). Education reform: A managerial agenda. *Phi Delta Kappan, 67,* 641-645.

Bolman, L. G., & Deal, T. E. (1993). *Reframing organizations: Artistry, choice, and leadership.* San Francisco: Jossey-Bass.

Carnegie Forum on Education and the Economy. (1986). *A nation prepared: Teachers for the 21st century.* New York: Author.

Conley, S. B., & Bacharach, S. B. (1990). From school-site management to participatory school-site management. *Phi Delta Kappan, 71,* 539-544.

Cooper, B. C. (1991). Changing paradigms of school organization: Implications of teacher collaboration on school operations. In S. C. Conley & B. C. Cooper (Eds.), *The school as a work environment: Implications for reform* (pp. 257-279). Boston: Allyn & Bacon.

Forester, A. D. (1991, October). *An examination of parallels between Deming's model for transforming industry and current trends in education.* Paper presented at the National Learning Foundation's TQE/ TQM Seminar, Washington, DC.

Frase, L. E., & Streshly, W. (1994). Lack of accuracy, commitment, and feedback in teacher evaluation. *Journal of Personnel Evaluation in Education, 8*(1), 140-143.

Holmes Group. (1986). *Tomorrow's teachers.* East Lansing, MI: Author.

Lortie, D. (1975). *Schoolteacher: A sociological study.* Chicago: University of Chicago Press.

Malen, B., Murphy, M. J., & Hart, A. W. (1987). Restructuring teacher compensation systems. In K. Alexander & D. H. Monk (Eds.), *Attracting and compensating teachers* (pp. 91-142). Cambridge, MA: Ballinger.

Malen, B., & Ogawa, R. T. (1988). Professional-patron influence on site based governance councils: A confounding case study. *Educational Evaluation and Policy Analysis, 10*(4), 251-270.

Marshall, C. (1992). *The cultural chasm between administrator and teacher cultures: A micropolitical puzzle* (Occasional Paper No. 12). Cambridge, MA: National Center for Educational Leadership.

Morgan, G. (1986). *Images of organization.* Beverly Hills, CA: Sage.

Sarason, S. B. (1993). *The case for change: Rethinking the preparation of educators.* San Francisco: Jossey-Bass.

Scull, R., & Conley, S. C. (in press). The school as a workplace: Making sense of multiple frameworks. *International Journal of Educational Reform.*

Willower, D. (1984). School principals, school cultures, and school improvement. *Educational Horizons, 63*(1), 35-38.

✧ 4 ✧

Fostering Continuous Improvement

The Japanese word for continuous improvement is *kaizen*. Continuous improvement reflects an ethos based on everyone's being responsible for getting better at whatever the group or organization does. Further, everyone has room for improvement, and the most successful schools, industries, and other organizations are those that embody the improvement ethic. The call for continuous improvement echoes throughout Deming's 14 points. Specifically, in this chapter we will address the following 8 of those 14 points:

2. Adopt the philosophy of cooperation instead of competition.
3. Cease dependence on inspection to achieve quality.
6. Institute training on the job.
7. Institute leadership—help people, equipment, and processes improve education continuously.
8. Drive out fear so that everyone can succeed.
11. Eliminate numerical goals and quotas—focus on doing a top-quality job at each step in the process.
12. Remove barriers to workers' pride of work—their sense of reward and satisfaction.
13. Institute a vigorous program of education and self-improvement. (Deming, 1986, pp. 23-24)

Point 7 captures the principal's primary mission. History tells us that the role of the principal has evolved from manager of buildings and grounds and enforcer of rules to judge of teachers; that is, the principal evaluates teachers yearly to determine their performance level and, supposedly, to assess their performance (Glickman, 1990). As we point out later in this chapter, the latter, performance assessment, has been a failed mission. One reason is that teacher evaluation has focused on mass teacher inspection (Point 3) to attain instructional excellence. Instead, principals and all school administrators need to provide continual resource assistance that teachers can use to upgrade their skills and further develop their careers. Administrators should continually work to remove barriers that prevent teachers from experiencing pride in their work and hence the sense of reward and satisfaction.

You may find it interesting that students have not yet been mentioned in this chapter. This reflects our belief that teachers must be customers, too—customers of principals. Individuals in every position in the school organization should view the next person as a client, ensuring that quality is delivered at every turn. Assistant superintendents should view principals as their customers or consumers, and continually ask, What can I do to help you do your job better? The same question should be asked by principals of their teachers, and teachers should ask the same of their students. Looking downstream, delivering quality, and helping others deliver quality are the keys. The age-old notion "You work for me" must be changed to "If we cooperate, we can do the best job possible." Competition has not lived up to its billing; far more frequently than not, it hurts people, the quality of life, and the quality of work (Kohn, 1986). The competitive mentality ignores the fact that the most effective schools are inherently collegial enterprises (Little, 1982).

As we discussed in Chapter 1, educating students is obviously the purpose of schools. Accomplishing the best education possible requires the cooperative efforts of teachers who serve the same clients (i.e., students). In Chapter 5, we discuss working together, breaking down barriers between people, and putting everyone to work as managers and leaders to accomplish TQE. In this chapter we focus on high-quality classroom instruction, the barriers that have limited it, and what must be done to attain it.

Focusing Teacher Evaluation on Professional Development

Professional development is one of the most powerful routes to teacher motivation and school improvement. Teacher evaluation is only one part of this goal. Its purpose should be to help teachers to improve systems and training so that everyone is successful and finds more joy in his or her work. Some elements of a useful evaluation program are as follows:

- An evaluation program should be built on the belief that teachers have a right to take joy in their work and evaluation should assist them in attaining this joy.
- An evaluation program should recognize that providing conditions (e.g., time and resources) in which teachers can share information about how they teach can foster a sense of personal satisfaction and professional development.
- An evaluation program should focus on developing and continuously improving quality of education by promoting teachers and principals and improving systems within the school and school district.

Teacher evaluation thus far has failed to include these elements, or to achieve any of the goals stated for it, except compliance with state laws. Teachers in Canada and the United States frequently find teacher evaluation useless (Frase & Streshly, 1994); it is hotly debated in the literature and understandably held in very low esteem by most teachers. In general, teacher evaluation has not led to improved instruction or elimination of less than competent teachers from the profession. Further, it is often taken lightly by administrators who lack adequate competence in the artful science of teaching.

Evaluation and supervision can lead to improved instruction, but not when these problems are present. Some school districts have demonstrated that teacher evaluation can lead to improved instruction; these include Catalina Foothills School District, Tucson, Arizona; Des Moines Public Schools, Des Moines, Iowa; Port Washington Schools, Port Washington, Washington; Kyrene Public Schools, Arizona; Poway Public Schools, Poway, California; and South Bay Public Schools, Imperial Beach, California.

In the pages that follow, we address the following six problem areas in teacher evaluation and recommend some practices administrators can use to overcome these problems in their schools:

1. Evaluation ratings are inflated or fail to provide valid data about employee performance.
2. Teachers receive little substantive feedback from evaluations for improvement.
3. Professional growth plans are generally absent or inadequate.
4. Many evaluations never take place.
5. Teacher evaluators lack adequate training.
6. Professional development is hit-or-miss, underfunded, and lacking in follow-up.

Until these problems are resolved, teachers and principals will continue to view evaluation as a practice with little value.

Inflation of Evaluation Ratings

It has been noted that evaluation ratings are inflated (Frase & Streshly, 1994; Langlois & Colarusso, 1988; White, 1990). In their classic text on organizational behavior, Porter, Lawler, and Hackman (1975), for example, cite evidence that performance evaluations fail to produce valid data about employee performance. The most common problems include the following:

- A "halo" effect, whereby a given employee tends to be rated identically on all evaluation items
- The fact that peers' ratings are often more accurate than superiors' ratings, but are seldom used

- The practice of some superiors' rating everyone high, whereas others tend to rate everyone low (p. 321)

These dysfunctional consequences are largely attributable to the fact that both evaluators and those to be evaluated approach performance appraisal sessions with much uneasiness. From the viewpoint of the inadequately trained evaluator, it is decidedly uncomfortable to be put in the position of evaluating teachers' performance and providing feedback. The process is similarly uncomfortable for the teacher being evaluated. Although he or she may desire feedback from the appraisal process, the teacher may have mixed feelings about receiving it, particularly if he or she feels that it is likely to be negative or unhelpful: "Subordinates don't want just any kind of feedback; they want *constructive feedback* that will help them reach their goals" (Porter et al., 1975, p. 320; emphasis added).

It is important to note that the above problems do not mean that performance evaluations cannot potentially lead to a number of positive consequences, such as the following:

- Valid performance data that can be used as a basis for rewarding employees, long-range planning, training, and career development
- Increases in both the intrinsic and extrinsic motivation of people who are evaluated
- The provision of constructive feedback that will help teachers improve their teaching
- A higher level of agreement between the administrator and the teacher about what constitutes good teaching, learning, and school improvement (Porter et al., 1975, p. 324)

In the remaining sections of this chapter we will discuss how these positive results might be achieved.

One of the authors has had a great deal of experience with the problems in school districts across the United States. During the past three years, he has been part of trained curriculum audit teams sponsored by the American Association of School Administrators who have gathered and analyzed probationary and tenured teacher evaluation data, teacher professional growth plans, and teacher and principal interview data in 10 school districts in the eastern and midwestern United States (Frase & Streshly, 1994). Teacher evaluation data from 1986 to 1993 were used in these studies. The number of students enrolled in these districts totaled approximately 200,000. In most of the districts, no teachers, including probationary teachers, were found to be below standard, and the large majority were rated well above standard. The skewing of these ratings toward the high side is illustrated in Figure 4.1.

The problem with inflation of ratings is not that a quota for inadequate teachers is not attained, for no quotas should exist. The problem is that the ratings do not represent reality. The teacher ratings found in this study are contradicted not only by research and public opinion, but also by auditors' observations of instruction in the districts mentioned and interviews with teachers and administrators. First, the auditors' observations revealed poor instructional practices, particularly in districts where the evaluation ratings were highest. The following are predominant examples:

- Exclusive use of drill and practice exercises
- Students' copying exercises and directions from books and workbooks
- Teachers not engaged with students (e.g., teachers with heads on desks; teachers grading papers, coloring posters, and doing other seat work while students complete rote exercises)
- Students asleep or inattentive in class
- Absence of lesson plans
- Use of low-quality and nonstimulating worksheets
- Students copying words from the chalkboard and/or copying definitions from a dictionary
- Teachers asking questions printed in a text and a very limited number of students raising their hands to answer
- Classes unattended by teachers

In general, learning activities were limited to low-level cognition only. The little direct instruction that did take place was oriented toward low-level cognition; teachers seldom interacted

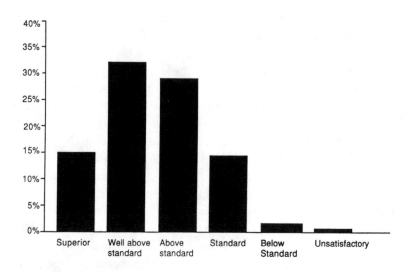

Figure 4.1. Distribution of Teacher Evaluation Ratings: A Sample From 10 School Districts

with students; little or no cooperative learning occurred; drill and practice were the predominant forms of instruction; and teachers demonstrated low expectations for student learning. These observations make it implausible that extraordinarily high percentages of teachers could be rated above standard or higher.

Interestingly, when asked about these instructional practices, teachers stated that they used them frequently. When asked the same question, the large majority of principals offered baseless and inaccurate responses, such as "These instructional practices are very solid" and "The teacher is doing a great job."

How can we use data like these? One interpretation we might make is the Tayloristic notion that the teachers are simply inadequate and must be coerced into performing better. The incorrect assumption here is that the cause is special: The teacher is simply inadequate. Another interpretation is that the teachers want to do a good job but need to improve their skills. A third is derived from Deming's belief that 85% of the problems in an organization are the fault of the system, not the people. In this interpretation the emphasis is on working with teachers to establish collegial relationships to improve the system, commonly agreed-upon goals, and the work environment. It may be that training is needed for skill improvement, but training is not the only focus. Much attention must be given to the work environment, an issue we explore in detail in Chapter 5.

Lack of Substantive Feedback
From Evaluations

As we noted in Chapter 1, a strong sense of teacher efficacy is very desirable, because it is related to student learning. Further, efficacious teachers have fewer student discipline problems. One way to enhance teachers' sense of efficacy is to provide them with helpful feedback, situation-specific feedback. The greater the amount of helpful feedback, the stronger the teachers' sense of efficacy (Azumi & Madhere, 1983).

A review of teachers' evaluations in curriculum audits nationwide has revealed very few suggestions for improvement. Those that were present were poorly done, offering only vague ideas for improvement, such as "Continue to work on math," or failing to relate to findings in the evaluation. Many did not address classroom instruction, but instead focused on committee work, outside reading, or exhortations to continue the great work. With this kind of feedback, along with the fact that the principal seldom comes into the classroom, rarely articulates a cogent point about instruction, has been known to ask for signatures on evaluations without having conducted observations, and frequently gives suggestions that do not make sense, why should teachers value teacher evaluation? Indeed, many teachers not only have no reason to value it, they have many reasons to discredit it as bureaucratic, legalized foolishness.

The following are examples of inadequate suggestions for improvement offered to teachers in the national study cited above:

- Use a variety of techniques and materials to sustain student attention.
- Each teaching episode should be better organized and structured.
- Become an effective classroom manager.

Each of these suggestions likely addresses something that particular teachers should do, but the problem is that the teacher probably already knows that these things should be done. Such feedback does not make a teacher feel good, and it offers no useful information. The teacher probably wants to do better. His or her most prized reward, helping young people learn, is not being attained. Teachers who are not achieving this goal may not express it, but deep down they are probably disappointed in themselves for not doing better. Following from Deming's assertion that 85% all problems in an organization are the fault of the system and not the worker, and the assumptions that teachers have the intrinsic motivation to help students learn and frequently are doing the best they know how to do, the TQE principal would ask the following questions:

- Has the teacher demonstrated effective classroom management techniques before? If so, the cause may be attributable to the system.
- Are system processes contributing to the problem? For example, are there inordinate numbers of students who have been discipline problems before in the class?
- If the system appears to be working, is there a skill deficiency problem on the teacher's part? If so, opportunities for professional development may be the answer.
- Has the teacher received opportunities to develop his/her classroom management skills? If not, development opportunities that address this skill area should be provided, and the training should be followed up.

Simply telling a teacher to "do better" is insufficient, pure and simple. It is as unreasonable as a mechanic expecting an engine that has a spark plug missing to run as effectively as a recently tuned engine. Teachers want to run effective classrooms. Exhortations and threats do not help; they only antagonize and intimidate. The teacher's question concerns *how* to run an effective classroom, not whether it should be done. Students need models, and so do teachers. Schools can provide models for teachers by (a) teaming teachers who need help with other teachers who practice effective classroom management, so that they can observe good practices and confer with each other; and (b) having principals provide demonstrations of proper techniques in the classroom.

A related problem exists when supervisors present feedback that is overly negative and critical. Porter et al. (1975) describe the effect of negative feedback, noting that employees often hear just the first few criticisms; they do not hear the rest because they are busy thinking up arguments to refute these criticisms. Similarly, Deming (1986) notes that most performance appraisal systems, particularly management by objectives and management by numbers, could be more appropriately termed "management by fear." Management by fear "nourishes short term-performance, annihilates long-term planning, builds fear, demolishes teamwork, nourishes rivalry and politics" (p. 102). Moreover, managing by fear explains why it is so difficult for staff to work together for the good of a company. Instead of managing by fear, the TQE principal encourages teachers and all staff to participate in the design of their work and evaluation processes, and to take creative risks.

Feedback is the breakfast of champions (Blanchard & Johnson, 1991). Everyone can grow with good feedback, but it must be palatable and presented in a caring, nonthreatening way.

Nonalignment of Desired Teaching Practices With Organizational Beliefs

Another interpretation of the problems in teacher evaluation is that they are a result of systemic organizational problems. The school district's evaluation system should not be viewed in isolation from other aspects of the organization. From Deming's point of view, this is one of the single biggest mistaken beliefs of managers. For example, a school could have the best evaluation system in the world, but if bureaucratic rules pervade the school and a sense of camaraderie is lacking between teachers and principal and among teachers themselves, a technically sound evaluation system will mean little.

Many readers may suggest that the teachers mentioned in the preceding section emphasize lower- rather than higher-order learning on the part of students, provide minimal student participation in lessons, and have low expectations for student learning. They might also suggest that such teachers are simply incompetent and must be coerced, through the evaluation process, into performing better. However, if we were to interpret these observations from a systemic point of view, we would use them not as a basis for drawing conclusions but, rather, for asking a number of questions:

- Are students' higher-order thinking skills emphasized within the school and the school district? If yes, is this emphasis reflected in the district's testing programs?
- Are teachers encouraged to experiment with their teaching and take creative risks? Is there tolerance for the possibility of failure from risk-taking behavior?
- Is every moment of the teacher's day prescheduled? Do teachers have time to interact with each other, to come up with new ideas and implement and monitor them? Are teachers' ideas for creative uses of time given serious consideration?
- Would teachers in the school say that their suggestions for their professional development as well as schoolwide improvement are acted upon?

We are suggesting that in schools where teachers seem to be using the same tried-and-true techniques with little active experimentation, it is inappropriate simply to evaluate teachers negatively. Rather, the entire school must be evaluated, with an eye toward making everyone in it more capable of constant experimentation and change. In Deming's interpretation, 85% of the problems in an organization are the fault of the structure of the system and not of the people. In this context the emphasis must be on working with teachers to establish collegial relationships to improve the system and the work environment. The evaluation system then becomes a part of a much larger systemic effort to improve the quality of the entire school.

Inadequacy or Absence of Professional Growth Plans

Hallmarks of an effective professional growth plan are clear goals set by administrators, the teacher, and colleagues. In the study of audits mentioned earlier, the auditors also reviewed teachers' professional growth plans, required by legislation in many states. In some states a teacher's plan must be designed by both the teacher and an administrator; in others, the teacher makes the plan and an administrator must approve it. The auditors found that legitimate professional growth plans do not exist for most teachers across the United States. Objectives for the growth plans they found lacked focus and specificity and were generally set by an administrator only. Some plans consisted of little more than "Complete an M.A. degree" and "Learn more about the new reading program."

In addition, most of the objectives that were specific and related to instruction were not aligned with improvement activities or evaluators' findings. For example, "increasing students' time on task" was stated as a goal for one teacher, but the supposedly related improvement activity was to become more familiar with the state curriculum assessment skills. Such misalignment was not an aberration in the national study. Most plans were not aligned with evaluation findings.

Giving constructive feedback to teachers is the principal's responsibility. Other teachers can and should also give such feedback. Studies have shown that the forms of in-service training that teachers value most are observation and consultation with other teachers, and individual study and research (Smylie, 1989). Exhibit 4.1 presents a checklist that can help enhance the quality of professional growth plans.

Checklist for Improving Professional Growth Plans

__ Professional growth goals and plans are specific and clear.

__ Professional growth plans are developed by the teacher, administrator, and colleagues.

__ Progress is monitored regularly by the teacher and principal.

__ Provisions are made for the teacher to observe other teachers, to be observed, and to talk frequently with expert colleagues.

__ The principal models the ethic and encourages teachers to seek advice when needed and to be receptive when advice is offered.

__ The principal provides discretion and autonomy to teachers to make classroom decisions with information about options.

Exhibit 4.1.

Lack of Evaluations

In one large metropolitan district, approximately 2,000, or 25%, of the observations scheduled never occurred (Frase & Streshly, 1994). They were not faked, they simply did not take place; this was on record, and no one expressed concern. Every administrator in that district who knew about this is guilty of malpractice. The numbers of evaluations never carried out in other districts were far lower, but the practice was somewhat neglected nevertheless. The principal's job is to provide, regularly and abundantly, rich and nourishing feedback, the breakfast of champions. Principals want to do this. We know of no principal who wants to do a bad or mediocre job. Everyone wants to do a good job and to feel the pride that follows.

Porter et al. (1975) coined the expression "the vanishing performance appraisal." Owing to the ambivalence felt by many evaluators and employees about performance appraisal in general, this phenomenon occurs in many organizations. In one study, employees in many lines of work reported that they had not had performance appraisals for several years, whereas superiors claimed they held regular performance appraisal sessions (Hall & Lawler, 1969; cited in Porter et al., 1975). The study discerned that although many superiors discussed performance with their employees in general terms, employees wondered why they were not getting the kind of feedback they wanted. Given superiors' mixed feelings about these sessions, it is not surprising that "what constitutes an acceptable appraisal session for an anxious superior might not provide the kind of information an [employee] wants" (Porter et al., 1975, p. 320). Exhibit 4.2 provides a few easy-to-follow steps that will help ensure that evaluations take place.

Lack of Adequate Training for Teacher Evaluators

When asked why they do not conduct timely observations and evaluations, the most frequent reasons principals offer are "I don't have time" and "I'm not sure it does any good." The first of these can be taken care of through proper establishment of priorities and more effective time management. The second will take more time and is more difficult. Among the audited districts, some provided and required no training; others required training of principals only when they first became principals. No district had a long-term plan for improving the evaluation or staff development system, or for providing evaluator training.

Principals and teachers who were interviewed confirmed the need for training. The fact that the principals lacked skill in evaluation gave teachers legitimate reason to believe evaluation was a waste of time. Principals, too, reflected their need and desire to become more skilled. The fact that they doubted that evaluations do any good is testimony to that fact. In districts where teachers are growing and learning, principals place a high value on the evaluation process. This is the heart of Deming's (1986) Point 13: "Institute a vigorous program of education and self-improvement"

Keys to Ensuring That Evaluations Take Place

__ The principal should make the observation schedule public and visible to all staff.

__ The principal should place all scheduled observations and conferences on his or her own and his or her secretary's calendars, and the principal's supervisor should receive a copy.

__ The principal should ask his or her secretary for reminders of all scheduled dates (observations and conferences).

__ The principal should remember that giving constructive feedback is as important as anything he or she does in the school.

Exhibit 4.2.

(p. 24). Ensuring that self-improvement programs are in place is the job of top management. It must become a priority; its importance must be demonstrated through modeling, and provisions must be made to enable others to do it. Exhibit 4.3 provides a checklist that superintendents and principals can use to ensure that the elements are in place for them to provide teachers with adequate feedback and development opportunities. These can be used to help meet the requirements of Deming's points 13 and 6.

The Hit-or-Miss Nature of Professional Development

The professional development systems in the districts audited and the findings from research on staff development generally reflect that professional development lacks planning, is a low priority in school district budgets, and generally involves a one-shot effort. Many of the districts in the study involved teachers in the development of professional improvement plans, but the involvement was superficial (Frase & Streshly, 1994). Active, meaningful involvement in teacher evaluation and professional growth offers a number of important advantages to teachers, principals, and schools in general:

- Evaluators are more likely to use a goal-setting system than a checklist system.
- Teachers are more likely to be committed to goals if they have had a hand in establishing them.
- Teachers will contribute meaningfully to the evaluation process.
- Teachers are more likely to feel that they have been appraised fairly if they have had input into the process.

The checklist in Exhibit 4.4 is based on successful experience and research in providing high-quality professional development programs. The checklist can be useful for determining the strengths of a program as well as areas needing improvement.

Summary

Teacher evaluation has a bad name, and it really is no wonder. Many administrators treat it with disrespect, it is sometimes used as a punishment and intimidation device, and evaluators are too often poorly trained. Hence constructive feedback that can help teachers make instructional improvement is greatly lacking. Further, too many problems are considered to be the fault of teachers when we know that in fact the majority are the fault of the systems in which teaching must take place. We summarize the six major points of this chapter below. Because of similarity in content, we have grouped some of them together.

- *Point 1:* The work environment and systems within which teachers and principals must work account for the majority of problems.
- *Point 2:* It is the responsibility of leaders to rearrange the system, with the help of others, to optimize the organization.

Checklist to Ensure Training and Self-Improvement

__ A strong statement that training and professional growth for every staff member are of paramount importance exists at the district office and in every school.

__ This priority is modeled by every administrator.

__ This priority is stated clearly as the purpose of the evaluation program.

__ It is clear in the district and school budgets that funds should be allocated every year for staff development, evaluation, and supervision.

__ It is public knowledge that all educational administrators must conduct demonstration teaching every year for teachers and administrators.

__ A monitoring system is in place to ensure that all aspects of the policy are carried out and working properly.

Exhibit 4.3.

To act on the above points, administrators should do the following:

Demonstrate these beliefs by encouraging teachers to look for better ways to do things.

Act on teachers' suggestions and assess the effects.

Model effective problem solving by bringing questions to teachers and seeking input.

- *Point 3:* Every person has room for improvement.

Administrators can make the most of this fact by taking several steps:

Demonstrate their own room for improvement by seeking and acting on consultation with teachers to improve the systems at work in the school.

Develop and complete your own professional growth plans and share it with the staff.

Checklist for Assessing Strengths
and Weaknesses of Training Programs

__ Money is budgeted and procedures are in place for encouraging teachers' attendance at conferences, conventions, and training and problem-solving sessions at the school site.

__ Opportunities are frequently available for teachers to observe other teachers teaching.

__ Reasonable, specific, and clear objectives and assessment strategies are written on what teachers will do in their classrooms as a result of each training program.

__ Teachers and principals work cooperatively to determine training needs and areas of desired study based on analysis of classroom performance.

__ Checkpoints are in place to ensure that training is based on need and research rather than fad.

__ Results are discussed and assessed by teachers and administrators.

__ Opportunities are available for follow-up consultations among teacher and administrators.

__ Each training session is evaluated by the principal and teacher, and the data are used to modify future development.

__ Adequate time is provided for training.

__ Support (time, material, and human resources) is provided for application of new teaching techniques or development plans.

__ Encourage group-based as well as individual professional development initiatives.

Exhibit 4.4.

Provide resources to support the professional development.

Discuss, frequently and openly, the ethos of continuous improvement of systems and people.

- *Point 4:* Feedback can be a healthy source of strength and direction for self-improvement and improved job performance.

Administrators must do the following:

Give constructive, helpful feedback frequently.

Give only honest feedback.

Seek feedback on their own performance.

Be specific in feedback; this builds credibility and thus the feedback has greater impact on the recipient.

- *Point 5:* Doing a good job is the greatest source of success, satisfaction, and internal motivation.
- *Point 6:* Teachers and principals want to do a good job.

Administrators can support the will to do a good job by doing the following:

Focus on and use intrinsic rewards, not exclusively on extrinsic rewards.

Focus on clearing the school environment of roadblocks that prohibit good teaching and learning—work continuously on improving the system.

In this chapter we have focused on continuous improvement and the belief that every person has room for improvement and the ability to improve. Individuals will admit this to themselves, but frequently will not admit it to others. This is not complicated psychology; it is a predictable reaction. It is predictable in that educators want to do a good job, and it is threatening and hurtful when they are told they are performing poorly. Getting over this hurdle, learning how to involve teachers and school administrators in improving their skills and fostering their professional development, is the job of the TQE leader.

A second major point regarding continuous improvement is the notion that, as Deming has observed, 85% of problems in an organization are the fault of the system, and only 15% are the fault of the people. TQE school administrators realize this and establish ways to involve teachers in improving the system. This is a quantum leap, a paradigm shift, for many leaders, because it means looking at the systems they have created, admitting that improvement is needed, and seeking the help of teachers and administrators in making improvements. In summary, TQE school leaders do not point fingers at others because they realize that when they do, other fingers are pointing at them. The TQE school leader begins the improvement process by addressing self-improvement first.

As we were putting the finishing touches on this chapter, we looked for a quotation that would summarize its message. We found it in *The New York Times* on July 20, 1993, where Robert B. Reich, U.S. Secretary of Labor, said it perfectly: "Our greatest weakness has been the failure *to invest adequately in our own learning.* In the emerging global, high-tech economy, the *development of our human resources will be the key means of creating wealth*" (emphasis added).

Key Terms and Concepts

Career development. The continuous process of further enhancing professionalism in one's career.

Constructive feedback. The information given to a professional by supervisor, peers, or self that highlights strengths, areas for improvement, and suggestions that may lead to improvement.

Kaizen. The Japanese word for continuous improvement.

Organizational beliefs. Values of the organization that are expressed verbally, in writing, or in practice. The key is whether verbal or written beliefs are in conflict with the organization's practice.

Professional growth plans. Plans developed by teachers and principals to enhance teachers' professional competence.

Ratings inflation. Inflation of evaluation ratings beyond reality.

References

Azumi, J., & Madhere, S. (1983). *Professionalism, power and performance: The relationships between administrative control, teacher conformity, and student achievement.* Paper presented at the annual meeting of the American Educational Research Association, Montreal.

Blanchard, K., & Johnson, S. (1991). *The one-minute manager.* La Jolla, CA: Blanchard-Johnson.

Deming, W. E. (1986). *Out of the crisis.* Cambridge: MIT Center for Advanced Engineering Study.

Frase, L. E., & Streshly, W. (1994). Lack of accuracy, commitment, and feedback in teacher evaluation. *Journal of Personnel Evaluation in Education, 8*(1).

Glickman, C. (1990). *Supervision of instruction: A developmental approach.* Needham Heights, MA: Allyn & Bacon.

Kohn, A. (1986). *No contest.* Boston: Houghton Mifflin.

Little, J. W. (1982). Norms of collegiality and experimentation: Workplace conditions of school success. *American Educational Research Journal, 19,* 325-340.

Langlois, D. E., & Colarusso, M. R. (1988). Teacher evaluation: No empty ritual. *Executive Educator, 10*(3), 32-33.

Porter, L. W., Lawler, E. E., & Hackman, J. R. (1975). *Behavior in organizations.* New York: McGraw-Hill.

Reich, R. B. (1993, July 20). Workers of the world, get smart. *The New York Times,* p. A19.

Smylie, M. A. (1989). Teachers' views of the effectiveness of sources of learning to teach. *Elementary School Journal, 89,* 543-558.

White, D. (1990, September 13). Nearly every Georgia teacher merits a raise. *Atlanta Journal and Constitution.*

✦ 5 ✦

Making the School a System

In the preceding chapters we have continually emphasized that school improvement and TQE are dependent on the active involvement of all stakeholders. The traditional view of "principal as manager" is no longer an adequate conception of school governance. Hardy and robust educational programs do not come from the principal acting alone as leader and decision maker. Contemporary management views and practices clearly state that principals must be leaders, but that leadership strength does not stem from the use of top-down control mechanisms. Schools are systems that must pull from the strengths of everyone involved. The key to school leadership is the facilitation of the participation of others in school improvement.

In this spirit, decisions are made according to a collegial or consensus model as opposed to an authority model. However, this consensus model does not simply mean that "majority rules." As one teacher association leader recently said to one of us, "Majority votes negate the interests of the minority." A consensus model strives to draw upon different interests rather than to negate any one interest. In this model, stakeholders air their different perspectives, viewpoints, and priorities for the purpose of devising and attaining common or mutually agreed-upon goals. A consensus model recognizes that the critical factor in any system consists of the relationships that emerge among people and how people jointly confront issues and decisions.

Decision Making on
Faculty and Administrative Teams

A teacher or principal who is part of a decision-making team or group that operates according to majority rule might first consider discussing with fellow team members the possibility of arriving at decisions through a consensus process. Such a suggestion might elicit some arguments—"We could never get everyone to agree on something!" "Meetings would take way too long!" "Someone has to make the decisions." All of these arguments have an element of truth. However, members might also consider a chief benefit of consensus decision making: If consensus can be formed, the feeling that there are necessarily winners and losers is often avoided.

One possible consensus technique for voting might be for members to select one of the following options when issues are being decided:

1. I strongly endorse this idea or issue.
2. I endorse this idea.
3. I see problems with this idea, but I will agree to a trial period.

This technique allows group members to dissent and to make their dissent known to others.[1] In this context, dissenting opinions should be documented in writing and should become part of "group memory." (For example, one of the authors uses butcher paper and magic markers for recording issues and decisions.) By the same token, if one or more members feel that they truly cannot live with an idea, the entire group will have a failed vote. Thus a potential downside to consensus decision making (or an upside, depending on your perspective) is that one member can block an issue from moving forward. However, we are suggesting that one way of minimizing this possibility is to invent a range of options rather than to pose a simple yes-or-no decision. This would allow a group member to say, for example, "I have problems with this idea, but I'm willing to go forward with it for two months—if the evaluation design addresses my concern and allows me and other group members to reassess progress at the end of the two-month period." In the following section we discuss a tool for monitoring group decisions more completely.

The Plan, Do, Study, and Act Cycle

Schools are notorious for forming plans, implementing them, and failing to assess their effects. It is no wonder many teachers complain, "Here comes another innovation—wait it out, and it too will pass!" Deming notes that this scenario is not unique to education. In fact, he suggests that plans should be implemented only if equally serious efforts are made to monitor the effects of those plans.

Deming's (1993) "plan, do, study, and act" (PDSA) cycle (see Figure 5.1) is a generic tool that people in a school system can apply to many different school improvement efforts to establish goals and monitor progress. The job characteristics model (JCM), developed by Hackman and Oldham (1980), provides one illustration of how the PDSA cycle might work in a school or school system to establish quality. The model provides decision makers with data about crucial elements of employees' jobs, those elements that are required before employees can find motivation and joy in their work and what Deming (1993) calls pride in workmanship.

The Job Characteristics Model[2]

Hackman and Oldham (1980) developed the Job Diagnostic Survey (JDS), which assesses an employee's perceptions of the job he or she performs. The survey is intended to provide managers with a way of ascertaining those elements of a job that could benefit from change as well as a model for implementing changes. The job characteristics model, upon which the JDS is based, posits that five "core" job characteristics foster three psychological states essential for maintaining motivation and experiencing satisfaction from one's work. These characteristics are skill variety, task identity, task significance, autonomy, and feedback from the work itself. The first three of these job characteristics are believed to

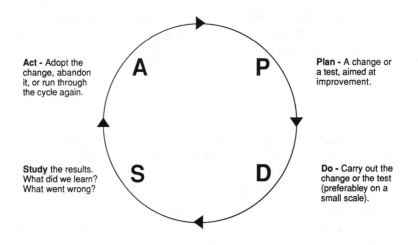

Figure 5.1. The Shewhart Cycle for Learning and Improvement: The Plan, Do, Study, and Act Cycle

SOURCE: Reprinted from *The New Economics for Industry, Government, Education* by W. Edwards Deming by permission of MIT and W. Edwards Deming. Published by MIT, Center for Advanced Engineering Study, Cambridge, MA 02139. Copyright © 1993 by W. Edwards Deming.

create the psychological state of "experienced meaningfulness," or the employee's perception that what he or she does is significant or important. The fourth job characteristic (autonomy) is thought to enhance the psychological state of "experienced responsibility," or the degree to which an employee feels responsible for work outcomes. The final job characteristic (feedback from the work itself) relates to the psychological state of "knowledge of results," defined as the degree to which the employee knows or understands the outcomes of his or her work. These three psychological states in turn contribute to "internal motivation," defined as the sense that an employee's feelings are directly tied to how well the employee performs on the job.

Hackman and Oldham (1980) then link these core dimensions to a set of action principles for redesigning jobs. This list, though not exhaustive, is representative of some of the principles that can underlie efforts to improve an individual's job:

- *Principle 1: Combining tasks.* This entails putting together existing fractionalized tasks to form new and larger modules of work.
- *Principle 2: Forming natural work units.* This involves arranging items of work into logical or inherently meaningful groups.
- *Principle 3: Establishing client relationships.* This involves forming natural work units around specific groups of customers or clients of the work.
- *Principle 4: Vertically loading the job.* This entails providing employees with increased control over the work by "pushing down" responsibility and authority that were formerly reserved for higher levels of management.
- *Principle 5: Opening feedback channels.* This means designing the job such that employees can learn directly how they are performing.

In the following sections we provide applications of the job characteristics model: the first at the micro, or individual teacher, level, and the second at the macro, or school and school district, levels. The five principles for redesigning jobs were used at both the micro and macro levels.

Work-Level Application

Two teachers, Betty and Anna,[3] were asked to respond to the items on the JDS. Betty is an Anglo female in her early 40s. She has been a teacher for 5 years, primarily of fifth-grade gifted and talented students. Anna is also an Anglo female in her early 40s; she has been teaching for about 12 years. Her teaching experience has largely been as a special education resource teacher, working with grades 4 through 6.

The JDS asks for responses to statements concerning a number of different aspects of the work, in accordance with the job characteristics described above. Respondents are asked whether a variety of statements about their jobs are accurate or inaccurate. The following is an example of an item tapping skill variety: "The job requires me to use a number of complex or high-level skills" (responses range from 1 = very inaccurate to 7 = very accurate). The JDS measures a number of work aspects in addition to these core job characteristics, psychological states, and internal motivation, including "growth need strength," or the degree to which an employee values opportunities for growth and development in the job, satisfaction with supervision, and feedback from others.

Figure 5.2 summarizes the responses for Betty and Anna on the five core job characteristics and also presents national norms for professional and technical job families provided by Hackman and Oldham (1980). With one exception, the scores for these two teachers are above national norms. The reader may note that Betty reports very low task identity, or the opportunity to engage in a "whole" task from beginning to end. This may reflect Betty's perception that her teaching work is fragmentary and incomplete. Hackman and Oldham might suggest that an attempt be made to redesign the job to provide Betty with more of a sense of complete teaching work. In accordance with Principle 1 (combining tasks), the job could be redesigned to provide opportunities for Betty to plan curricula with the sixth-grade gifted and talented teacher or with other fifth-grade regular education teachers.

Betty's growth need strength score is also low when compared with national norms for this job category (i.e., 3.5 compared with a national norm of 5.1; not shown in Figure 5.2). This finding indicates that the design of the job may not be the sole issue, and that internal forces of the individual must be addressed as well. Indeed, further investigation of Betty's work situation revealed that she is transferring to a middle school position, where she will teach social studies and language arts at a new grade level while also instructing gifted and talented students. (This new position may provide Betty with a greater sense of combined tasks and "whole" and complete work.) Anticipating this change, she may feel that she has maximized her instruction of fifth-grade curriculum and enrichment and is therefore unenthusiastic about opportunities for growth and development in her current (but not necessarily her future) job.

Anna's job characteristics scores are all above national levels (see Figure 5.2). The job thus appears to provide Anna with ample skill variety, autonomy, a sense of work significance, feedback from the job, and complete work. However, Anna is significantly below

	Skill Variety	Task Identity	Task Significance	Autonomy	Feedback from job
Betty	6.6	3.3	7.0	5.6	5.6
Anna	7.0	6.0	7.0	6.3	5.6
National Norms 1	5.4	5.1	5.6	5.4	5.1

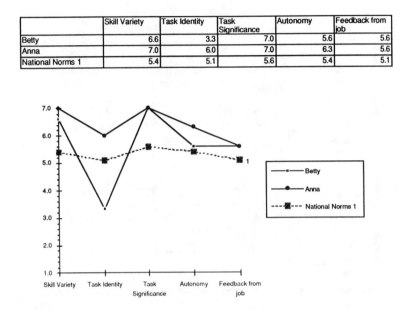

Figure 5.2. JDS Profiles for Betty and Anna, and National Norms

NOTE: National norms are for professional or technical workers (Hackman & Oldham, 1980).

national levels on three additional work features measured by the JDS: feedback from others, satisfaction with supervision, and growth need strength (1.0, 2.3, and 4.6, respectively, compared with national norms of 4.2, 4.9, and 5.1; scores not shown in Figure 5.2).

Further investigation of Anna's work situation revealed that she is experiencing a great deal of frustration stemming from her sense of work isolation. Her classroom is in a portable building located away from the mainstream school population. Although the school has 650+ students and 30+ classroom and resource teachers, Anna's contacts with other teachers and the principal are sporadic and infrequent. As a resource teacher, she has a different schedule from those of self-contained classroom teachers, and she consequently has only intermittent contact with other teachers. In addition, meetings with classroom teachers are normally held to discuss

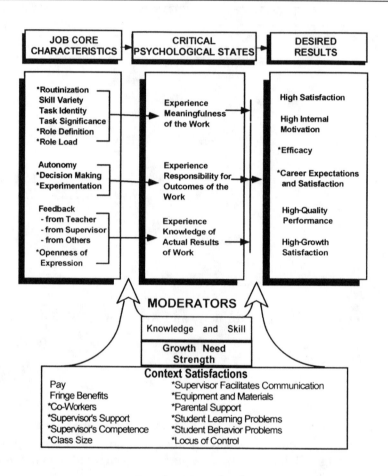

Figure 5.3. Modified Job Characteristics Model
(Adapted from Frase & Heck, 1992)
* = Additions.

problems occurring in the classroom only; work accomplished in the resource room is seldom discussed, and Anna feels that some teachers are not even aware of what their students are doing there.

Through the application of Hackman and Oldham's action principles—namely, Principle 2 (forming natural work units), Principle 3 (establishing relationships with clients), and Principle 5 (opening feedback channels)—Anna's job might be redesigned to alleviate the discrepancies that exist. Rather than pull students out of their regular classrooms to go to a resource room, the students might remain in their classrooms while the resource teacher provides small-group or individual instruction using the lesson being taught to the other classmates. Regularly scheduled meetings might be planned between the resource teacher and grade-level teachers to discuss progress and develop congruent instructional strategies for students. With the resource teacher working in the classroom, there is an increased chance that he or she would receive feedback from the principal. A schedule could then be coordinated between the principal and teacher for additional interaction and the provision of feedback from that interaction.

From the administrator's point of view, the JDS can be a valuable proactive tool. Not only does it indicate areas of discrepancy between the scores of individual teachers and national norms, it also makes it possible for the administrator to identify whether patterns of concern may exist among the faculty as a whole. It is this instance to which we turn in the following section.

School-Level Application

The modified job characteristics model (MJCM) is a revision of the JCM that includes job characteristics of particular importance to teachers (Frase & Heck, 1992; Matheson, Frase, & Heck, in press). These additions include decision making, opportunities to experiment, opportunities to express self, and teacher efficacy. These are noted by asterisks in the MJCM presented in Figure 5.3.

The Modified Job Diagnostic Survey (MJDS) includes survey items to measure the additions to the model. The survey items were derived from the surveys used in the original research. The MJDS is completed by teachers, and the scores reflect their perceptions. The 38 topics addressed in the MJDS are shown in Table 5.1.

TABLE 5.1. Topics Addressed in the Modified Job Diagnostic Survey

	Range of the Scale
Critical psychological states	
1. experience meaningfulness of work	1-7
2. experience responsibility of outcomes of the work	1-7
3. experience knowledge of actual results of the work	1-7
Job core characteristics	
4. skill variety	1-7
5. task identity	1-7
6. task significance	1-7
7. autonomy	1-7
8. feedback from teaching	1-7
9. feedback from supervisor or others	1-7
10. Motivating Potential Score (MPS)	125-200
Personal work outcomes	
11. high satisfaction	1-7
12. high internal motivation	1-7
13. career intentions (12.1)	1-4[a]
14. high-quality performance (13)	1-7
15. high growth satisfaction	1-7
16. efficacy	1-7[a]

Designing the Project

The MJCM and MJDS have been used for work environment improvement in the Fort McMurray Catholic Schools (FMCS) in Fort McMurray, Alberta, Canada. This work is directed at the school and district (macro) levels and focuses on the essence of TQE, creating good places to work, where teachers can experience

TABLE 5.1. Continued

	Range of the Scale
Context satisfaction	
17. pay	1-7
18. coworkers	1-7
19. supervisor support	1-7
20. competence	1-7
21. class size (14.1)	1-4
22. student learning problems	1-4[a]
23. student behavior problems	1-4
24. supplies (14.7)	1-4[a]
25. parental support (14.4)	1-4[a]
26. prep time (24.1)	variable
27. communication (15.11)	1-7
28. teaching assignment (15.10)	1-7
Bureaucracy	
29. routinization	1-4[a]
30. role ambiguity	1-4[a]
31. role overload (18.1)	1-5[a]
32. involvement in decision making	1-5
Interactive work context	
33. openness of expression	1-5
34. encouragement of experimentation	1-5
35. principal facilitates teacher interaction	1-5
36. career expectations (22.1-22.4 average)	1-4[a]
37/38. present/would like summary (average)	1-7

a. Indicates a lower score is desirable for the construct.

pride in their work. Consistent with Deming's belief that the transformation is everyone's responsibility, the district named the committee the Yours, Mine, and Ours Committee.

"Creating a good place to work" for teachers has been the motto of the FMCS project. By conventional standards, the schools in the FMCS system are good places to work: The salary schedule is the highest in Alberta, fringe benefits are second to none, facilities are immaculate, and yearly studies have revealed healthy school climates. However, the teacher turnover rate varied around 30%, and student test scores, although good, were not indicative of the community's potential for achievement. With this in mind, the Yours, Mine, and Ours Committee chose to focus on the motivation potential present in each school. Specifically, the committee asked whether the job characteristics present allow teachers to find job motivation.

The district chose the MJDS as the instrument for gaining an in-depth analysis of each school as a workplace. The MJDS yields a score for the exact feature the committee chose for its focus, the Motivation Potential Score (MPS). A high MPS means that the key job characteristics are available for teachers to find enhanced motivation for their work. However, the actual motivation must come from the person; the job characteristics provide only potential. Further, the MJDS offers a score for each of the characteristics in the MJCM (see Figure 5.3).

Implementing the Project

The project has followed a yearly PDSA cycle for 5 years. Teams were formed at each school to direct the project. After the MJDS was administered, committees from all schools received scores for all characteristics and their schools' MPSs. These scores were provided each year to each school team. The PDSA cycle consisted of the following steps:

- Diagnose by administering the MJDS at each school and analyzing the data.
- Develop intervention strategies at each school to improve scores for selected job characteristics.
- Implement intervention strategies at each school.

- Assess changes by administering the survey and analyzing the results.
- Revise as needed.

Results

The results for the first four years at the district level are presented in Figure 5.4. The MPSs indicate a large improvement from Year 1 to Year 2. It is likely that this was caused, at least in part, by the Hawthorne effect (see Frase & Heck, 1992). However, the results of the next two administrations of the MJDS confirmed the institutionalization of the effects. Note that the MPS declined slightly from the second to the third year, although it was still well above the first year (see Figure 5.4). In the fourth year, the MPS made additional gains and rebounded. At the district level, 22 of the 38 variables produced statistically significant gains across the four years of the study (Matheson et al., in press). MPSs for all schools across the four years are presented in Figure 5.5.

These macro- or district-level analyses can be useful to school boards in conducting yearly assessments of districts, but they offer few usable data to individual school principals and teachers. For school-level use, scores for each characteristic in the MJCM were given to school teams consisting of administrators and teachers at the school. Per the PDSA cycle in Figure 5.1, the teams analyzed data and developed intervention strategies to improve the respective conditions. The effects of one school's efforts for three years are illustrated in Figure 5.6. Some of the notable effects include the following:

- Statistically significant gains in teachers' perceptions of the following:
    - Experiencing meaningfulness of work (bar 1)
    - Experiencing responsibility for outcomes of work (bar 2)
    - Identification of tasks (bar 5)
    - Degree of autonomy (bar 7)
    - MPS (bar 10)
    - Supervisor competence (bar 20)

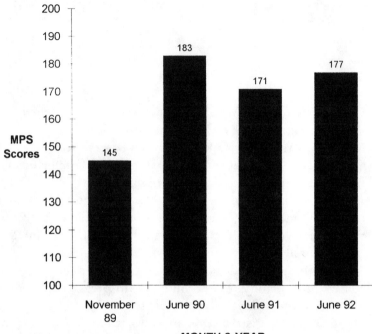

Figure 5.4. Fort McMurray Catholic School District's Yours, Mine, and Ours Committee: Motivation Potential Scores

Decrease of role ambiguity (bar 30)
Involvement in decision making (bar 32)
Encouragement of experimentation (bar 34)
Reduction in difference between present (bar 37) satisfaction levels and "would like" (bar 38) satisfaction levels

• Although not statistically significant, gains in teachers' perceptions of the following:
Feedback from teaching (bar 8)
Feedback from supervisor or others (bar 9)
Increase in job satisfaction (bar 11)
Increased satisfaction in professional growth (bar 15)
Increase in teachers' sense of self-efficacy (bar 16)

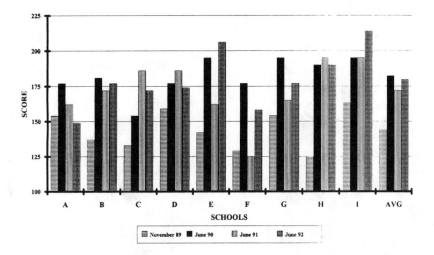

Figure 5.5. Fort McMurray Catholic School's Yours, Mine, and Ours Committee: Job Characteristics Study to June 1992, Graph 10, Job Core Characteristics–Motivation Potential Scores

Decrease in role overload
Principal's facilitation of teacher interaction

Intervention Strategies

The intervention strategies employed to make these gains in teachers' perceptions of their work and work environment varied. Data for one school indicated that the teachers perceived their principal's instructional competence as low. Another school's data indicated that the teachers wanted the principal to spend more time in their classrooms. These were difficult data for the team (principals and teachers) to deal with, because they appeared demeaning. The key was for the teams to use the data as constructive feedback. Everyone believed that everyone else wanted to do the best job possible. With that basic belief, the teams worked together to find time-use strategies that would allow the principal to spend more time in classrooms, and they specified the kind of instructional assistance teachers wanted from the principal so that additional training could be taken.

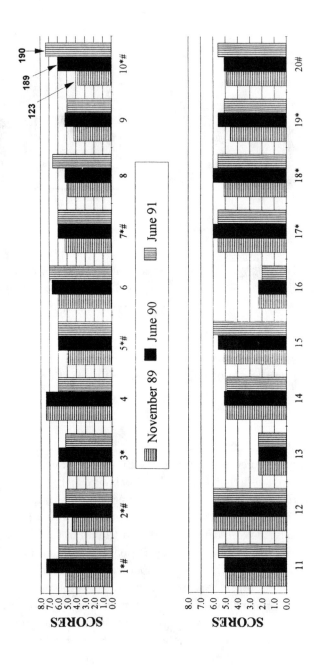

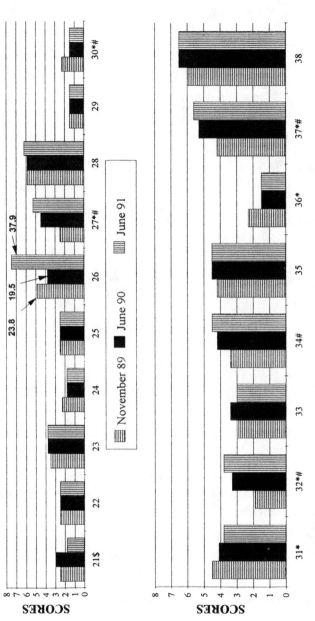

Figure 5.6. Fort McMurray Catholic School's Yours, Mine, and Ours Committee: Job Characteristics Study to June 1991, Comparison of November 1989, June 1990, and June 1991, Indicators for St. Anne

* Significant difference between the November 1989 and June 1990 surveys (alpha = .05).
\# Significant difference between the November 1989 and June 1991 surveys (alpha .05).
\$ Significant difference between the June 1990 and June 1991 surveys.

Other interventions involved redesigning school decision-making strategies, providing time to reflect on student progress, and designing teacher activities to identify tasks more clearly and to gain feedback from teaching.

Summary

The original JCM and JDS and the MJCM and MJDS are crucial tools in building TQE work environments that allow teachers to experience pride in their work (Deming, 1993). Further, when these tools and processes are utilized with the quality renewal system, teacher' skills and careers are enhanced, yielding greater joy in work and enhanced internal motivation to pursue the teachers' number-one goal—to help young people learn.

Key Terms and Concepts

Authority model. A decision model that prescribes decisions to be made by people within power positions, without consideration of consensus; reflected in top-down management styles.

Consensus model. A decision model that requires consensus of stakeholders' opinions.

Intervention strategies. Strategies used to redesign jobs to gain improved scores on the MJDS.

Job characteristics model (JCM). A causal model showing the relationships between key job characteristics and desired outcomes in an organization.

Job Diagnostic Survey (JDS). A Likert-type scale survey used to measure workers' perceptions of all items in the JCM as they apply to their workplace.

Job redesign. Redesign of jobs in an organization based on findings from workers' responses to the JDS.

Modified job characteristics model (MJCM). A revision of the JCM that includes key factors known to affect teachers' motivation and satisfaction, based on educational and psychological research literature.

Modified Job Diagnostic Survey (MJDS). A revision of the JDS that includes survey items used to assess the factors taken from the educational and psychological research that were added to the JCM to create the MJCM.

Motivation Potential Score (MPS). The score derived from workers' responses to the JDS; reflects the potential of the workplace to motivate workers.

Plan, do, study, and act (PDSA) cycle. A TQM procedure for instituting organizational improvement in quality.

Notes

1. We are grateful to Justo Robles for this idea. For additional information on site-based decision-making see National Educational Association, 1988.

2. We are indebted to Jonathan Becker for his contributions to both the discussion of Hackman and Oldham's model and the cases for the work redesign illustration. These cases were initially prepared by Jonathon Becker for a class taught by Sharon Conley at the University of Arizona.

3. These names are pseudonyms.

4. Measures for career satisfaction, routinization, role ambiguity, student learning problems, and student behavior problems were adapted from Bacharach, Bauer, and Conley (1986) and Conley, Bacharach, and Bauer (1989).

References

Bacharach, S., Bauer, S., & Conley, S. (1986). Organizational analysis of stress: The case of elementary and secondary schools. *Work and Occupations: An International Sociological Journal, 13*(1), 7-32.

Conley, S., Bacharach, S., & Bauer, S. (1989). The school work environment and teacher career dissatisfaction. *Educational Administration Quarterly, 25*(1), 58-81 .

Deming, W. E. (1993). *The new economics for industry, government, education.* Cambridge, MA: MIT Center for Advanced Engineering Study.

Frase, L., & Heck, G. (1992, February). Restructuring in the Fort McMurray Catholic Schools. *Canadian School Executive,* pp. 3-9.

Hackman, J. R., & Oldham, G. R. (1980). *Work redesign.* Menlo Park, CA: Addison-Wesley.

Matheson, R., Frase, L., & Heck, G. (in press). A story of praxis: Practice informed by theory. *Canadian School Executive.*

National Education Association. (1988). *Employee participations programs: Considerations for the school site.* Washington, DC: Author.

❖ 6 ❖

Creating Learning Places
for Teachers, Too:
An Epilogue

The ultimate goal is to bring improved performance, quality, and output to education, and, simultaneously, to bring pride of workmanship to teachers.

(derived from Deming, 1986, p. 248)

The notion of bringing pride of workmanship to teachers is the heart of TQE. We know that people are the most valuable resource in any organization. For example, witness the differences between the former USSR and Japan. The former was large, with abundant material resources, whereas the latter is small (about the size of California) and lacking in any significant material resources. Which is more successful? This is a foolish question—the Japanese people have a far higher standard of living and have been a powerful economic force in the world. Compare that to the former USSR; it was militarily powerful, but economically drained to the point of its recent demise. The crucial difference lies in how the two view productivity. We know the stories of both; the differences are obvious. Further, we know that the Japanese have taken major market shares from the United States. The key difference has been and is found in varying definitions of quality, and that difference hinges on the role of people in the workplace, which is what this book is all about. This book is about TQE, treating teachers as customers, and bringing pride of workmanship to them.

The TQE school is different from others. It recognizes and treats all of its clients equally as customers. It recognizes that teachers and administrators come to the profession with the goal of helping young people learn. It recognizes that their biggest reward and most powerful motivator is success in achieving that goal. Teachers are held responsible for developing and maintaining dynamic and creative learning environments for their students. This is a reasonable responsibility, given adequate resources, training, and a supportive work environment. The TQE school provides these. The TQE administrator realizes it is foolhardy to think that teachers can live up to their responsibility without receiving the same level of care and attention.

The TQE school recognizes that the systems and procedures with which teachers and administrators must work are responsible for a large majority of the school's problems, and the people themselves are responsible for only a few. It recognizes that high-quality work is dependent on *continual* correction of the problems in the systems and a focus on maximizing the professionals' opportunities to achieve success. It realizes that this is the only way to achieve optimization. Leaving any aspect out will yield suboptimization only.

The TQE principal recognizes the necessity of working with teachers to foster continuous improvement of both the teachers' and the principal's skill and career development. TQE administrators realize their responsibility to be in classrooms, at least half of the school day, observing and working with teachers to solve curriculum and instructional systems and problems. TQE administrators recognize the crucial importance of constructive feedback on instruction and make arrangements whereby teachers can provide each other with feedback on instruction. TQE administrators are continually improving their own instructional abilities and work at offering accurate, constructive feedback to teachers. TQE principals model this behavior by presenting lessons for teachers' critiques and then seeking and openly accepting constructive feedback. Further, TQE principals seek and act on feedback from customers (students, teachers, parents, and community) regarding their performance as principals.

The TQE school has a specific, participation-derived mission, and it sticks to that mission, marshaling its resources to achieve it. Likewise, the TQE school realizes that it cannot be responsible for mitigating all problems created by society. Violence, racial and social inequality, deteriorating values, poverty, and illiteracy are society's problems, and the school is just one institution. The larger society must accept responsibility for its own condition. Education must stop accepting the blame for society's many problems and must stop taking sole responsibility for correcting them. This is not to minimize the importance of the problems; it is simply to say that the school, teachers, and adminstrators cannot do it all. When the school takes on too many missions, nothing is done well, and quality suffers. Mary Nebgen, superintendent of the Reno Public Schools, has conveyed this message very well: "I am being asked to correct the economic state in which some of our students live. I can't do that. I can't fix all that. I can't provide long-term family counseling. There has to be some societal acceptance of responsibility" (quoted in Ehrenhalt, 1993, p. 68).

TQE school leaders, teachers, and principals take control. They have an internal locus of control and a strong sense of efficacy. Further, they work independently with others while applying profound knowledge in decision making. They share profound knowledge with each other and external customers and seek to build everyone's leadership capabilities. As Belasco and Stayer (1993) illustrate, geese take turns leading, flying at the tip of their V formation. The effective leader is a lead goose, one who knows when to let others lead. In contrast is the style of the lead buffalo—when the lead buffalo is not leading, the herd stagnates and accomplishes little, waiting for the leader to return. TQE schools are filled with leaders who understand their roles as leaders and as participants.

The TQE school is built on the belief that there are many leaders in it. The TQE principal's role is to establish a working environment in which teachers and students can be successful. Constancy of purpose toward this end is sacred, and it is everyone's responsibility.

Key Terms and Concepts

Pride of workmanship. The feeling of reward gained from doing high-quality work. The TQE school concentrates on establishing a working environment where workers can optimize their pride in their work.

References

Belasco, J., & Stayer, R. (1993). *Flight of the buffalo.* New York: Dove/Warner.

Deming, W. E. (1986). *Out of the crisis.* Cambridge, MA: MIT Center for Advanced Engineering Study.

Ehrenhalt, A. (1993, August 4). Malaise and America's schools. *Education Week, 12*(40), 68.

✧　　✧

Planning and Troubleshooting Guide

Teachers as Customers

DATE DUE

GAYLORD			PRINTED IN U.S.A.